Prayer Odyssey

A JOURNEY TO LIFE-CHANGING PRAYER

Prayer Odyssey

A Journey to Life-Changing Prayer

Dave Earley

Treasure House

An Imprint of

Destiny Image₀ Publishers, Inc.
P.O. Box 310
Shippensburg, PA 17257-0310

"For where your treasure is, there will your heart be also."
Matthew 6:21

ISBN 0-7684-2955-2

For Worldwide Distribution

Printed in the U.S.A.

This book and all other Destiny Image, Revival Press, MercyPlace,
Fresh Bread, Destiny Image Fiction, and Treasure House books are available
at Christian bookstores and distributors worldwide.

1 2 3 4 5 6 7 8 9 / 09 08 07 06 05 04

For a U.S. bookstore nearest you, call
1-800-722-6774.

For more information on foreign distributors, call
717-532-3040.

Or reach us on the Internet:
www.destinyimage.com

DEDICATION

To Bert Earley, My Mom

In the later years of her life she became a pint-sized dynamo of intercessory prayer who has impacted and continues to impact many lives, especially mine.

ACKNOWLEDGMENTS

There are many people I need to thank for shaping my life of prayer and for helping make this book a reality.

I am extremely grateful for the giants who led the way in prayer: John Wesley, Charles Finney, George Muller, Andrew Murray, Brother Lawrence, E. M. Bounds, Frank Laubauch, Madame Guyon, John R. Rice, and S. D. Gordon. Thanks to my modern era teachers Richard Foster, Elmer Towns, Jerry Falwell, Jack Hayford, Dick Eastman, Ted Haggard, Harold Vaughan, Peter Wagner, John Maxwell, Vernon Brewer, Bruce Wilkerson, Wesley Duewel, and Tommy Tenney.

I deeply appreciate the "mighty men" who hold up my hands in prayer daily. I cannot name all fifty of you, but we know who you are. Although I must mention Rod Bradley as he is the "mighty man" of the "mighty men".

I am indebted to my co-laborers and teammates at New Life—Steve Benninger, Brian Robertson, Susan Chittum, Jim Strong, Ron Vining. You are the "big five".

I am very grateful to Don Milam and the Destiny Image staff who minister out of lives vibrant in prayer. Thanks to Steve Coffey for giving me an opportunity to first teach this information when it was just an idea.

I want to especially thank my precious family who believe in me when no one else does.

ENDORSEMENTS

"Dave Earley is one of the best communicators I have heard. His ability to bring practical insight and understanding to deep spiritual principles has impacted my life and the lives of countless others around the world. Once again, in his new book, *Prayer Odyssey*, Dave brings powerful yet practical insights on a subject that is so vital today."

—Don Moen
Executive VP/Creative Director, Integrity Media

"With the glut of books on prayer available in the marketplace, it would seem near to impossible to say anything fresh on the subject. Pastor Dave Earley has accomplished the next to impossible! Writing in a very accessible style, he offers warm, exceptionally practical counsel for moving into more mature realms of prayer. This is not a book of theory; rather, Pastor Earley has given us a practical spiritual guide written by an obvious practitioner of prayer. Not only is the book refreshing and practical, it will also change your spiritual life forever! One cannot follow the principles of this book without becoming more deeply in love with Jesus Christ."

—Rich Nathan
Senior Pastor, Vineyard Church of Columbus

"I've known Dave Earley for almost a quarter of a century. In those years, I've watched a man who consistently lives what he teaches when it comes to seeking God through intercession. So much of Dave's growing influence in the Body of Christ is the result of his prayers and the prayers of others on his behalf. The church he leads was birthed in prayer—and to this day is prevailing because of prayer. This isn't a book on theories about prayer, or just a list of great ideas on intercession; it's a book that reflects years of Dave being in a spiritual laboratory, alone with God, experiencing His presence, and delighting in His glory."

—Dr. John D. Hull
President, EQUIP International, Coauthor of *Pivotal Praying*

"A lovely journey into life-changing prayer! This book will open many levels of prayer to the reader. It will be useful for personal growth and also for small groups to experience ancient patterns for communicating with the Master."

—Ralph W. Neighbour, Jr.

"Dave Earley is one of the outstanding graduates of Liberty University who has built more than just a super church; he has built a spiritual church. That is because his church is built on prayer and fasting. *Prayer Odyssey* is a book that tells how you can journey into the heart of God through prayer. It tells how you can know God intimately and get answers to your prayers."

—Jerry Falwell
Pastor
Thomas Road Baptist Church

"Dave Earley is offering practical means for the pursuit of a more vibrant, constant renewing prayer life. Every believer worth "the salt" Jesus called us to be wants this, and here is food to nourish that hunger."

—Jack W. Hayford
Chancellor
The King's College & Seminary

"I have known Dave Earley for over twenty years, first as a student, then as a church planter, and now as a mega-church pastor. The greatness of his ministry has always been rooted in his prayer life. As a student he fasted for ministry, as a church planter he fasted for growth and evangelism, and now as a mega-church pastor he fasts for multiplied impact on his metropolitan area in Columbus, Ohio. This book, *Prayer Odyssey*, comes from the heart of one who knows how to find the heart of God."

—Elmer L. Towns
Liberty University

"This work of creative non-fiction will transform your prayer life and relationship with God."

—Dr. Howard G. Hendricks
Distinguished Professor
Chairman, Center for Christian Leadership, Dallas Theological Seminary

"I know Dave Earley personally as a man who has been used of God to build a very large and spiritually healthy church from nothing. During the nine years he has ministered in our city, he has been a humble man who depends on prayer as his key to life and ministry. This book will be a rich feeding for those hungering for deeper experience in prayer, from a man who knows what he's talking about."

—Dennis McCallum
Xenos Christian Fellowship

"In a time when prayer is practiced in so many inappropriate ways, understanding biblical prayer is essential. Going beyond the question of the "why" of prayer, Dave Earley leads us in a personal discovery of how Scripture is foundational to prayer in all aspects of life! Our workers around the world have been challenged and inspired to grow deeper in their prayer life through the truths found in this book!"

—Steve Coffey
International Ministries Director ,Christar

"Prayer Odyssey is an extremely practical, helpful, readable challenge to grow in prayer. Dave Earley pastors a strong church that selflessly reaches out to people, even 'the least.' They joined our team in reaching thousands of inmates in prison. I want to see this pivotal book on prayer in prisons, homes, and for that matter, everywhere."

—Bill Glass
Former All Pro, Cleveland Browns
Founder, Weekend of Champions Prison Ministry

CONTENTS

Introduction

THIRTY-ONE FLAVORS

Taste and see that the Lord is good (Psalm 34:8).

"Here it is," my dad said as we pulled up in front of a crumbling brick building located just off the downtown section of our small town. I had just turned nine years old and was on my way to my first job interview. I followed my dad into a large, cold room furnished with only a worn, army-green, metal desk and a wooden swivel chair. In the chair sat a bald, round man happily chewing on his cigar. My father walked me up to the desk and introduced me to my new boss, Mr. Fee, the man in charge of the paperboys.

Fee shook his head. "He looks pretty small to me. Are you sure he can handle it?"

"He can handle it," Dad said.

Thus began my career as a paperboy. I delivered papers after school every day, and on Sundays my dad got up and helped me deliver the much larger Sunday papers.

There were many things I did not like about being a paperboy, things like big, barking dogs, people who never seemed to be able to come up with the money to pay me, and delivering papers in the rain. But the one thing I *did* like was that each day after I delivered my last paper I rode my bike home past the local Baskin Robbins ice cream shop. (As you may recall, Baskin Robbins boasts of offering 31 flavors of ice cream.) So after I delivered my last paper in the afternoon, I would stop in and have a strawberry ice cream cone.

Everything was going well until one day disaster struck. As usual, after I had delivered my last paper, I popped in the door of Baskin Robbins. However, this time when the man behind the counter saw me, he sadly shook his head. "Sorry kid," he said. "No strawberry today. We ran out and won't get any more for a while."

I must have looked like I was going to cry because he quickly added, "But don't worry. We have 30 more flavors. Why don't you try butter pecan?"

So I did. I reluctantly took my first lick of the honey-colored ice cream with soft brown nuts. My taste buds stood up and applauded. "Dreamy—it is so smooth and creamy!"

The next day I tested watermelon ice. My taste buds sent the report to my brain, "So refreshingly moist and light; tart yet sweet. A must-have on a hot day! Guaranteed to refresh you all over."

Then I tasted blackberry. "Wow!" (I even said it backward, "Wow!") It was a lot like strawberry except it had more of a kick.

The next day I got brave and took a stab at peach melba. "Zowwy! It was so good…just the right amount of sweet and tart blended together."

Each day as I delivered papers on my route I would joyously consider what flavor I would explore when I was finished. What new taste adventure lay ahead? Thirty-one flavors! I could not believe my good fortune. I found myself on a 31-flavor ice cream odyssey and was having a marvelous time.

But, when I was on only flavor number 8 or 9 in my joyous journey through all 31 flavors, it all came to a sad and sudden halt. I ran out of money and could not collect from my customers for several more weeks.

And Dad did not give advances for ice cream.

———— ⊰◉⊱ ————

Prayer that connects us with God is like ice cream, only so much better. Ice cream is a glorious treat, but prayer is infinitely more glorious than ice cream could ever hope to be because prayer connects us with God. God is infinitely tasty, wondrously good, marvelously awesome, and supremely sensational. God-connecting prayer is the basis for the great adventure into the manifold "flavors" of God.

The past few years I have been on a powerful, personal, prayer odyssey through a variety of types of prayer. Each type has its place and its merit. The goal of this book is to lead *you* on a prayer odyssey in order to deepen and strengthen your relationship with God. If you apply what you read, you will find your prayer life to be wonderfully expanded and renewed as you learn to approach God in fresh ways. It is a journey that could change your life!

Before beginning to look at the many types of prayers discussed in the *Prayer Odyssey*, let me first offer five simple truths that are important for you to remember.

First, there are many types of prayer. Ephesians 6:18 speaks of praying "all kinds of prayers." We do not know how many kinds of prayers there are, but certainly more than 31. (I have defined almost 50 types of prayer.)

Baskin Robbins has *more* than 31 flavors of ice cream—but they offer only 31 flavors at a time. This book gives only 31 of my favorites, but there are many more. God is infinite; so how could we put a number on the types of prayers we can bring Him? You may have a favorite that is not addressed in this book. That's great. Every time I teach on the 31 types of prayer someone comes up afterward to tell me of one I left out. This book is designed to not only teach you my favorites, but also encourage you to discover your own.

Second, the 31 "flavors" of prayer are not rigid. They often overlap and flow into each other. Like ice cream, they may taste better mixed together with another flavor. Many people like chocolate and peanut butter mixed together as one flavor. In a similar fashion, you may like to mix two or more flavors of prayer in one session of prayer. For example, this morning I enjoyed an hour in prayer and used six different flavors, about 10 minutes each.

Third, there are some flavors you will use more often than other flavors. You may find yourself using some flavors every day. Some are more for special seasons and situations of life. This will become obvious as you enjoy them. Also, as we tend to do with ice cream, you may tend to go with one flavor for a while then switch to another. I used to eat only strawberry ice cream; then my favorite became butter pecan, then peach melba. So it is with the types of prayer.

Fourth, because there are 31 types of prayer covered in this book, you might like to read about a new one each day for a month as part of your time with God. The chapters are short and are designed to be easy to read. You may go in order or jump around as the situation demands. I tend to jump around and use the type or types I need most that day.

Fifth, and most important, the flavors of prayer are made to be enjoyed. Ice cream was not made to be studied—it was made to be eaten. Similarly, prayer exists for our enjoyment. Dig in. Don't read this book like a textbook; instead use it to prompt you into a fresh approach to relating to God. As you enjoy new types of prayer, I believe that you will experience fresh depths of delight in your relationship with God.

Let this book help take you on your own prayer odyssey. The chief end of man is to love God and enjoy Him forever. Therefore, use the 31 flavors of prayer to enjoy God more than ever and to take a prayer odyssey that will change your life.

Part 1
Daily Prayers

Chapter 1

SPECIAL INTIMACY PRAYER

Imagine the thoughts that went through his mind that day. He was exhausted and hungry, and he smelled like a pig. He had been away from home so long…too long. Sure, he missed the warm meals and having his own bed, and the steady work and resulting allowance were definitely nothing to scoff at. But there was one thing he missed much more than all of that. He missed Father.

Over and over he had heard Father's voice in his head. It was deep, but warm. Many times that voice had a laugh in it, but was never frivolous. It spoke words of unerring wisdom. But best of all, Father's voice was always full of love, even on the day he left.

Why did he have to say what he had said that day? "Give me my share." He could tell his arrogant departure speech had hurt Father deeply. How he would love to take back every stupid word. But it was too late for that. He had made a fool of himself, had wasted his inheritance, and worst of all he had hurt Father.

The best he could do now was to go back and say, "I have sinned against heaven and against you. I am no longer worthy to be called your son; make me like one of your hired men."

So he went back to his father's house and the most amazing thing happened:

But while he was still a long way off, his father saw him and was filled with compassion for him; he ran to his son, threw his arms around him and kissed him (Luke 15:20).

Jesus told us this story to show us the Father heart of God. It teaches us one of my favorite types of prayer. I call it special intimacy or *Abba* prayer.

The word *Abba* is an Aramaic term used in the Bible to describe the unique relationship granted to believers under the new covenant. It is the most intimate term available to express a child's tender relationship with his or her father, and as such was used only by children. It is translated as "Father" or "Daddy." It is a personal word that moves prayer into the realm of deep intimacy as shown by Jesus when, in deep agony at the Garden of Gethsemane, He unburdened His soul to His Father in Heaven (see Mark 14:36).[1]

Abba prayer is the special privilege of the New Testament saint (see Rom. 8:15-16; Gal. 4:5-6). In the Old Testament believers were not allowed such personal access to God. They certainly were not encouraged to call Him "Father," let alone "Daddy." According to Professor Joachim Jeremias, "There is not a single example of the use *abba* in the whole of Jewish literature."[2]

Special intimacy prayer is the way a child of God approaches our heavenly Father. It is crawling into the Father's lap to receive His love, comfort, healing, and strength. It is taking our heavenly Daddy's hand and walking a while. Special intimacy prayer is more than prayer of the lips or of the mind. It is the deep prayer of the heart. It is crying out to the Father to be your Father and to "father" you through a difficult season of life. It is bringing your prodigal soul home to God and experiencing the Father running to you, throwing His arms around you, and giving you a hug and a kiss. It is enjoying the same privilege of intimacy with the Father that Jesus the Son experienced in the flesh.[3]

<hr/>

"Father, please 'father' me. I feel like a lost, little boy. The world is more than I can handle. I am supposed to be the one with the answers and I don't have a clue. Everyone needs me to be the parent right now, but I need permission to be your little boy for just a few minutes. Daddy, father me."

This was my prayer. I was buried under the stress of being the pastor of a large church. My three teenage sons were at the natural stage of life where they were pulling away from their mother and especially needed me to father them through adolescence. I felt the terrible tug of having to parent both my children and aged parents. My mom had just passed away. My dad needed me. My wife's father was dying. I was overwhelmed with feeling like I had to be everyone's "parent."

So I practiced the joy of special intimacy prayer…and a wonderful thing happened. I felt the reassuring hug of God around my weary soul. I sensed Him saying, "You'll do fine. I am with you all the way."

One Sunday I was speaking on the prodigal son and special intimacy prayer in my church. As I spoke, I found myself nearly overwhelmed with a passion that everyone would experience what I had known in special intimacy prayer. My voice quaked as I spoke of the Father running up to us, putting His arms around us, and kissing our cheeks. I was startled by the boldness in which I asked the audience if they had ever known the hug and kiss of God. One of our members sat on the fourth row with a deep frown etched on her face.

Afterward this wonderful, mature believer came to me with her complaint. "I have never had such an intimate experience with God. It makes me uncomfortable when you talk about being hugged and kissed by God."

I waited for a rebuke. But she surprised me when she dropped her head and asked, "Will you pray for me?"

I put my arm on her shoulder and prayed, "Father, this is Your daughter. She has served You so faithfully and diligently for many years. You love her more than she can possibly imagine. I ask that in Your way and in Your time that You would reveal Your fatherly love for her on a deeper level than she has ever known. Let her experience Your hug."

Wiping tears off her cheeks she walked away.

The next Sunday I saw her approaching. The moment I saw her I knew.

"Pastor Dave," she said through dancing eyes. "Now I know what you mean when you talk about being hugged by the Father. This week I got my hug. The rest is more than words can express."

I wonder. Have you ever gotten a hug from God? Do you know what it means to feel the Father's loving arms around you? Have you ever sensed His tender kiss on your cheek?

Have you truly experienced the Father love of God? Have you ever felt the freedom to call God, "Daddy"? Do you know what it is like to lose your little hand in His great big hand? Have you heard His warm voice saying, "There, there My child. It will be all right. Father is here. Let Daddy take care of it."

When was the last time you snuggled up in the Father's lap?

At times, prayer is simply crawling into Daddy's lap. He has a big lap and plenty of room and love for you there.

Quietly, picture yourself crawling up in the lap of your heavenly Father. Feel His strong arms around you. Know that you are in the place where you are loved completely.

Let the troubles of the day disappear in the power of His presence. Tell Him all about everything that happened to you today.

Feel free to sigh, smile, cry, or just listen to the thump of His heart beating with yours.

Thank Him for loving you enough to be your heavenly Daddy. Slowly allow yourself to be drawn into deeper prayer, worship, rest, and love.

ENDNOTES

1. William Hendricksen, *New Testament Commentary: Exposition of Paul's Epistle to the Romans* (Grand Rapids, MI: Baker Books, 1980), p. 259.

2. Joachim Jeremias, *The Prayers of Jesus* (Philadelphia, PA: SCM, 1967), p. 11.

3. Richard Foster, *Prayer: Finding the Heart's True Home* (San Francisco, CA: Harper Collins Publishers, 1992), p. 135.

Chapter 2

SOLITUDE PRAYER

What a busy, draining day! Jesus got up that morning and went to the synagogue and taught the people. As Jesus taught with authority, a demon-possessed man cried out, "What do You want with us, Jesus of Nazareth? Have You come to destroy us? I know who You are—the Holy One of God!" (Mark 1:24)

Jesus cast out the demon and freed the man from his agony. Then Jesus and some of His disciples went to the house of Simon Peter's mother-in-law. She was sick in bed with a fever. Jesus healed her, and she got up and fixed them a meal.

News of the freeing of the demon-possessed man and the healing of Peter's mother-in-law spread all afternoon. By evening the people began to line up with sick and demon-possessed people. Mark 1:33 says the crowd was so large that "the whole town gathered at the door." Jesus was busy late into the night healing the sick and freeing the demonized.

Now that's a draining day of teaching, healing, and casting out demons! I would have been exhausted. Yet, as I read this passage in Mark's Gospel, what is amazing to me is not Jesus' long day, but what He did the next morning.

Now in the morning, having risen a long while before daylight, He went out and departed to a solitary place; and there He prayed (Mark 1:35 NKJV).

How did Jesus combat the fatigue of a draining day of ministry? He practiced solitude prayer. Notice carefully what He did:

"In the morning...a long while before daylight." Jesus chose a solitary time.

"He went out and departed." Jesus chose a solitary act to distant Himself from people for a time.

"To a solitary place." Jesus chose a solitary place.

"*He prayed.*" Jesus used solitude from people as a sanctuary to God and He prayed.

Jesus got away *from* others so He could get away *with* the Father. He sought physical solitude in order to address His spiritual needs. He not only got still before God, He got alone with God. He practiced solitude prayer.

This was His secret for staying fresh, sharp, full, centered, and on-track. During His three-and-a-half years of intense ministry He used solitude to keep His spiritual tanks full and His emotional batteries charged.

Don't we need to learn to do the same?

You may be thinking, *Yeah, but He was the Son of God.*

And I say, "Yes, and if the Son of God needed to practice solitude prayer, *how much more* do you and I? If the Son of God needed to get up early and go to a solitary place and pray, *how much more* do you and I?"

The sad reality is that most of us are too busy, too crowded, and too cluttered to stay spiritually sharp, full, charged, and optimally useful to God, others, or even ourselves. Most of us have lives filled with too much activity, too much noise, and "too much people" for us to have very much left for God. Our lives are so full of stuff—good stuff, perhaps, but still "stuff"—that there is little room for God. All of us must learn the art of solitude prayer.

Solitude prayer is shutting ourselves away *from* people so we can shut ourselves away *with* God. It is escaping the sound of human voices so we can hear the voice of God. It is the voluntary abstinence from our normal patterns of activity and interaction with people for a time in order to rediscover that our strength and well-being come from God alone.

Henri Nouwen has noted, "Without solitude it is virtually impossible to lead a spiritual life."[1] Why is this so? Because in solitude we are freed from our bondage to clatter, clutter, and crowds so we can hear, feel, touch, taste, and know God. In solitude we learn to let go of all else so that we might grab hold of God. We find a healthy detachment from the world and a special attachment to God.

Solitude prayer is an essential secret of spiritual freshness, fullness, centeredness, and strength. I know I desperately need those graces, especially spiritual strength. Isaiah gives us insight about how to derive strength from God.

Have you not known? Have you not heard? The everlasting God, the Lord, the Creator of the ends of the earth, neither faints nor is weary. His understanding is unsearchable. He gives power to the weak, and to those who have no might He increases strength. Even the youths shall faint and be weary, and the young men shall utterly fall, but those who wait on the Lord shall renew their strength; they shall mount up with wings like eagles, they shall run and not be weary, they shall walk and not faint (Isaiah 40:28–31 NKJV).

Notice that in verse 31 the secret of great mental, emotional, spiritual fortitude is with those who "wait on the Lord." This "waiting" involves time and speaks of place. The spiritually strong are those who have a time and place for solitude prayer.

Jesus not only practiced solitude prayer, He encourages us to practice it. He spoke of going into our "closet" so that the God who sees in secret may reward openly:

But when you pray, go into your room, close the door and pray to your Father, who is unseen. Then your Father, who sees what is done in secret, will reward you (Matthew 6:6).

Have you formed the holy habit of meeting with God daily in quiet time and in the secret place? Those people who could be called spiritual successes; those who have developed spiritual depth; those who have tasted and seen that God is good; those who have run and not grown weary and walked and not fainted; those are people who have practiced one thing above all others. They have established the habit and discipline of a daily time alone with God in His Word and in prayer.

I have found that one of the most important questions I can ask people to determine their spiritual potential and future is this: When and where do you meet God daily? Without exception, the individuals who can answer this question with a solid answer do well. The others are going to struggle.

Let me encourage you to carve out a special time of secret and solitude with God on a consistent basis. Maybe it will be first thing in the morning. Possibly it will be late at night. Maybe it will be at midday. It could be at the dining room table. Possibly it will be in your car on the way to work. Maybe it will be in your bedroom. Perhaps it will be as you walk in a nearby park. The time and place are not as important as the fact that you have a time and a place for secret/solitude prayer. Pick a time. Choose a place. Get started today.

ENDNOTES

1. Henri Nouwen as quoted by Richard Foster and James Bryan Smith in *Devotional Classics* (San Francisco, CA: Harper Collins Publishers, 1990), p. 95.

Chapter 3

SIMPLE PRAYER

When I was beginning high school I was very confused and unhappy. I was running from God and disgusted with myself. Despair and loneliness dominated my thoughts. Thankfully God kept after me. Eventually, in my junior year I got tired of fighting against God and I quit running. I stopped and committed my all to God.

One of the most wonderful results of committing my life to God was the great joy in knowing I had discovered an awesome secret friend. Prior to coming to God I had felt lonely. But now I was never alone. I could think of and quietly talk with God all day long. Everything became an object of prayer. Every place became a place of prayer. No matter where I went, I could hang out with God. He is omnipresent and had been there before, but now I was keenly aware of His presence. I felt it.

It was so much fun developing my familiar friendship with Jesus. I liked my other friends, but in so many ways He was so much better. He was smarter than the rest of us. He understood how I really felt, even when I did not. And He was always there.

I woke up in the morning chattering to God because He was there. I would come back to Him again and again throughout the day because He was there. I talked with Him silently as I walked through the hall and cried out to Him as I jogged or hiked in the woods after school because He was there. Drifting off to sleep I thanked Him for all He did for me that day because He was there. It was not complex. It was all very simple. Later I discovered that my prayer life was what some Christian mystics call "simple prayer" and others refer to as elements of contemplation or meditation.[1] I did not know or care what it is called, I simply enjoyed having a friend who was always there.

——— ·((()))· ———

Simple prayer is an ongoing and growing relationship with God. It is carrying on a never-ending conversation with God about the daily stuff of life. It is chattering away to the Father about all of our thoughts, events, hurts, sorrows, joys, and questions freely and openly because He listens. It is sanctifying the ordinary by turning all of the ordinary events and experiences of daily life into prayer.

In college I came across a little book called *The Practice of the Presence of God*. A man named Nicholas (who was later known as Brother Lawrence) wrote it. He was a very large and awkward man who was always breaking things. His job was washing pots and pans and cleaning a large kitchen. Yet he loved God with all his heart. He set a goal for himself to practice the presence of God all day long. This continual practice of the presence of God is the essence of simple prayer.

Nicholas discovered that the way to sense God's presence all day was to have lots of conversations with Him. In fact he thought it was shameful to cut off a conversation with God. His goal was to form the habit of talking to God all the time. The key was continually loving God and recognizing Him as intimately present with us, and therefore addressing Him with every thought.[2]

I am not sure I have attained the continual conversation with God advocated by Brother Lawrence, but I do enjoy simple prayer. I love the days when I seem to be thinking about and talking to God all day long. I thank Him for this and praise Him for that. I ask for help with one task and wisdom for another. I pray for this person and rejoice over God's work in another. And it is fun!

I have tried to build some habits into my life that trigger simple prayer. Whenever we get in the car we pray short prayers about where we are going and what we are going to do. Whenever I walk the dog the first thing I do when I walk out the front door is repeat the Lord's Prayer. When I go through all my Emails at work, I like to pray a simple prayer regarding each one.

The days I help out with my son's paper route I pray through the ACTS of prayer (A: adoration, C: confession, T: thanksgiving, and S: supplication) as I walk the route. At mealtime we always thank God before we eat. As I lay in bed I try to thank God for the events and answers of the day. And I cast all my cares upon Him.

Let me encourage you to make today a day of simple prayer. Try to go through your day with the persistent awareness of the presence of God. Carry on a never-ending conversation with God about the daily stuff of life. Chatter away to the Father about all of your thoughts, events, hurts, sorrows, joys, and questions freely and openly because He listens. Sanctify the ordinary by turning all of the ordinary events and experiences of daily life into prayer.

ENDNOTES

1. Thomas Merton, *The New Seeds of Contemplation* (New York, NY: New Directions, 1961), p. 1.

2. Brother Lawrence, *The Practice of the Presence of God* (Grand Rapids, MI: Baker Book House, 1975).

Chapter 4

SECURING WISDOM PRAYER

Talk about big shoes to fill. Wow! King David was a dashing, intelligent, handsome, larger-than-life living legend. He was a military hero, songwriter, folk legend, spiritual leader, wise governor, and powerful king. He had killed Goliath, eluded Saul's army, recruited a band of merry men, become the king, led the tiny nation to become a world power, wrote the Psalms, created the "Bathsheba-gate" scandal, survived an ugly military coup plotted by his own son, and planned to build God a great temple. And now his son Solomon had to step up and take his place.

What Solomon needed is what all of us in positions of responsibility need: wisdom. So he approached God with a humble heart and asked for wisdom. First Kings and Second Chronicles record his prayer:

"Now, O Lord my God, You have made Your servant king in place of my father David. But I am only a little child and do not know how to carry out my duties. Your servant is here among the people You have chosen, a great people, too numerous to count or number. So give Your servant a discerning heart to govern Your people and to distinguish between right and wrong. For who is able to govern this great people of Yours?" (1 Kings 3:7-9)

That night God appeared to Solomon and said to him, "Ask for whatever you want Me to give you." Solomon answered God, "You have shown great kindness to David my father and have made me king in his place. Now, Lord God, let Your promise to my father David be confirmed, for You have made me king over a people who are as numerous as the dust of the earth. Give me wisdom and knowledge, that I may lead this people, for who is able to govern this great people of Yours?" (2 Chronicles 1:7-10)

Notice his requests, *"Give your servant a discerning heart to govern Your people and to distinguish between right and wrong"* (1 Kings 3:9) and *"Give me wisdom and knowledge, that I may lead"* (2 Chron. 1:10). What does Solomon do when facing overwhelming responsibility? He prays a securing wisdom prayer.

Securing wisdom prayer is asking God to give you wisdom to lead. It is humbling yourself and realizing that you do not have the answers. It is asking God to give you discernment to know what is right. It is seeking direction as you make decisions affecting those under your responsibility.

This request for wisdom is the type of request God loves to answer. And God did answer Solomon in an unbelievable fashion. First Kings records God's response:

The Lord was pleased that Solomon had asked for this. So God said to him, "Since you have asked for this and not for long life or wealth for yourself, nor have asked for the death of your enemies but for discernment in administering justice, I will do what you have asked. I will give you a wise and discerning heart, so that there will never have been anyone like you, nor will there ever be" (1 Kings 3:10-12).

Second Chronicles records the Lord's answer with these words:

God said to Solomon, "Since this is your heart's desire and you have not asked for wealth, riches or honor, nor for the death of your enemies, and since you have not asked for a long life but for wisdom and knowledge to govern My people over whom I have made you king, therefore wisdom and knowledge will be given you. And I will also give you wealth, riches and honor, such as no king who was before you ever had and none after you will have" (2 Chronicles 1:11-12).

Soon after this, two prostitutes came to Solomon to get a ruling. They lived in the same house and both had newborn children. The first woman claimed that the second woman's baby had died in the night and the second woman had switched her dead baby with the first woman's living baby while the first woman slept. The second woman claimed that this was not true. Solomon had to decide who was right.

Solomon ordered a man to cut the living baby in half and give each woman a half. The first woman cried out, "Give her the baby. Don't kill him!"

The second woman said, "Neither of us will have a living baby. Cut him in two."

Solomon smiled and wisely ordered, "Give the baby to the first woman. She obviously is the real mother" (see 1 Kings 3:16-28). The fame of Solomon's wise decision spread throughout the nation.

The Book of First Kings summarizes the amazing way God answered Solomon's prayer for wisdom:

God gave Solomon wisdom and very great insight, and a breadth of under-standing as measureless as the sand on the seashore. Solomon's wisdom was greater than the wisdom of all the men of the East, and greater than all the wisdom of Egypt. He was wiser than any other man, including Ethan the Ezrahite—wiser than Heman, Calcol and Darda, the sons of Mahol. And his fame spread to all the surrounding nations. He spoke three thousand proverbs and his songs numbered a thousand and five. He described plant life, from the cedar of Lebanon to the hyssop that grows out of walls. He also taught about animals and birds, reptiles and fish. Men of all nations came to listen to Solomon's wisdom, sent by all the kings of the world, who had heard of his wis dom (1 Kings 4:29-34).

Solomon is now known as one of the wisest and richest men who ever lived. He wrote the Books of Proverbs, Song of Solomon, and Ecclesiastes. God certain-ly answered his prayer for wisdom.

The securing wisdom prayer is not reserved for Solomon or just some rare individual. The Book of James gives all of us the encouragement to ask for wisdom.

"If any of you lacks wisdom, he should ask God, who gives generously to all without finding fault, and it will be given to him" (James 1:5).

One of the 31 flavors of prayer I use most often is the securing wisdom prayer. I have three teenage sons and I lead a large church with a couple dozen employees. It seems like I need to make an important decision or give someone necessary advice every day. So I ask for wisdom and God helps me.

Are there some decisions you need direction in making? Are you trying to figure out how to lead your family? Do you need insight into a relationship? Do your job responsibilities require you to make decisions that affect the livelihoods of other people? Are there other areas where you need wisdom? Let me encourage you to try securing wisdom prayer. Why not pause right now and ask God to give you wisdom for each decision you encounter and each area you're responsible for?

Chapter 5

SUCCESS PRAYER

Thousands of years ago, a man faced a very difficult assignment. It all began when his boss, Abraham, was 140 years old. Abraham's wife, Sarah, had recently passed away. Abraham desperately wanted his son, Isaac, to marry and give him a grandson, but Isaac was 40 years old and still single. So Abraham took action.

Abraham called in his chief servant and gave him a very difficult assignment. (Many Bible scholars believe this servant was Eliezer, the servant whom Abraham trusted enough to consider making his heir in Genesis 15:2-3.) Abraham asked him to travel 450 desert miles by camel to the area from which Abraham had come. There he was supposed to find a suitable bride for Isaac from among Abraham's distant relatives. (The custom at that time was to marry a first cousin.) After finding such a girl, he then would have to convince her to return with him to marry a man she had never met. This was a very difficult assignment.

The servant gathered a small caravan and made the long trek to Abraham's homeland. His plan was to find the right girl at the central meeting place for desert communities, the well. As he approached the town, he offered a simple prayer:

> *Then he prayed, "O Lord, God of my master Abraham, **give me success today**, and show kindness to my master Abraham. See, I am standing beside this spring, and the daughters of the townspeople are coming out to draw water. May it be that when I say to a girl, 'Please let down your jar that I may have a drink,' and she says, 'Drink, and I'll water your camels too'—let her be the one You have chosen for Your servant Isaac. By this I will know that You have shown kindness to my master"* (Genesis 24:12-14).

The servant prayed, "Give me success today." This prayer was short and personal, and definite in reference to time. He wanted God to lead him to the right girl and do it right away. Abraham was very old and Isaac was not getting any younger. In order to know which girl was the right one the servant added to his request that she not only offer him a drink, but also offer to water his camels. He prayed a success prayer and God answered.

> *Before he had finished praying, Rebekah came out with her jar on her shoulder. She was the daughter of Bethuel son of Milcah, who was the wife of Abraham's brother Nahor. The girl was very beautiful, a virgin; no man had ever lain with her. She went down to the spring, filled her jar and came up again. The servant hurried to meet her and said, "Please give me a little water from your jar." "Drink, my lord," she said, and quickly lowered the jar to her hands and gave him a drink. After she had given him a drink, she said, "I'll draw water for your camels too, until they have finished drinking"* (Genesis 24:15-19).

Wow! God answered his prayer and then some. *Before he had finished praying,* God sent the right girl in the right way. As he would later find out, she was a relative of Abraham. The Bible describes her as a very beautiful virgin. Beyond that, she not only gave him a drink, but also offered to water his camels! That's not all. Later on we read that she was willing to leave with him right away. And best of all, when Isaac met her, he immediately loved her (see Gen. 24:58-67).

This servant's prayer for success became a life-changing blessing for everyone involved. Rebekah's life was radically changed as she left home and family to live 450 miles away. She was blessed with a husband who loved her and was given a place in the lineage of the Messiah.

Isaac's life was changed because he received a bride, and a very beautiful one at that. She would be the woman he would love and who would bear his sons.

However, I think that the one most influenced by this prayer was the servant himself. Prior to this event, he viewed God solely as "Abraham's God." He did not have a very personal relationship with the Lord. Yet, when he saw the loving and powerful way God answered his prayer, he became a man with a firsthand relationship with God, who worshiped God for himself.

Then the man bowed down and worshiped the Lord, saying, "Praise be to the Lord, the God of my master Abraham, who has not abandoned His kindness and faithfulness to my master. As for me, the Lord has led me on the journey to the house of my master's relatives" (Genesis 24:26-27).

His life was changed to such an extent that he became an excited witness to others. He eagerly told Rebekah's older brother all the Lord had done for him (see Gen. 24:34-48). In his excitement he spared no detail.

Success prayer is asking God to give you success in a task you believe God wants you to accomplish. It is doing your part and asking God to do the rest. It is being willing to stick your neck out expecting God to come through for you.

Many of us tend to hold back. We think God's promises and great answers to prayer are for some super saint and not for us. But I think this story reminds us that praying for success is for everyone who wants to give God the glory. The servant in this story was unnamed. Although we might conjecture that the servant was Eliezer, we do not know. In Genesis 24 he is simply called "the chief servant" of Abraham. Since nothing in the Word of God is written the way it is written by accident, I think the servant is unnamed to remind us that prayer is for everyone. All of us can be a servant and see God answer our prayers.

It is so encouraging to realize that if God would answer the prayer of this unnamed man who had only a secondhand relationship with God, then *how much more* will He do for us! We are His children. We call Him "Abba Father." We do not have to be "big-name Christians" to see God answer our prayers.

———— ❈ ————

Abraham's servant is not the only one who prayed the success prayer when facing a difficult assignment—so did Nehemiah. Nehemiah realized that God had positioned him to fulfill the impossible task of rebuilding the walls around Jerusalem. In order to have any hope of succeeding he would need to convince

King Artaxerxes to grant him permission to leave his post as the king's cupbearer and, more importantly, to supply him for both the journey back to Jerusalem and with the materials he needed to rebuild the walls. Notice what he prayed:

O Lord, let Your ear be attentive to the prayer of this Your servant and to the prayer of Your servants who delight in revering Your name. Give Your servant success today by granting him favor in the presence of this man." I was cup-bearer to the king (Nehemiah 1:11).

This success prayer was wonderfully answered (see Neh. 2:8). This success prayer and God's answer of it became a source of great encouragement for Nehemiah when he encountered opposition. He even mentions it in responding to the "naysayers."

I answered them by saying, "The God of heaven will give us success. We His servants will start rebuilding, but as for you, you have no share in Jerusalem or any claim or historic right to it" (Nehemiah 2:20).

The success prayer is a simple little prayer that can yield big blessed results. Let me encourage you to ask God to give you success when you begin a new day and before each new assignment. When you sense that there is a task God wants you to accomplish, do not be afraid to ask God to give you success. He did it for Abraham's servant. He did it for Nehemiah. He has done it for countless others. And He can do it for you.

Part 2
Growth Prayers

Chapter 6

SAYING "THANKS" PRAYER

We don't know if they were surprised to see Jesus or if they had arranged it ahead of time. The Bible does not tell us. It does tell us that ten lepers met Jesus when He was traveling along the border between Samaria and Galilee on His way to Jerusalem. (See Luke 17:11-19.) Regardless of whether the meeting was planned or not, the adrenaline that must have shot through their systems at seeing Jesus would have been extreme.

Henry David Thoreau, a 19th-century writer, said that all men live lives of quiet desperation. These ten lepers could certainly attest to that. As lepers these men were cursed to live lives of total isolation and humiliation as well as public desperation. They were outcasts. They were forbidden to touch another person out of fear that their disease might spread. And there was no known cure for their leprosy. Gradually it would consume more and more of their limbs, until death was a welcome relief.

When they saw Jesus on that road they saw in Him a slim ray of hope in their dark, desperate future. He had the reputation of being a healer. They had heard that He had already healed one leper (see Matt. 8:2). Maybe, just maybe, He could heal them.

So they did the only thing a desperate soul can do. They prayed.

"Jesus, Master, have pity on us!"

And He did!

Jesus healed them! We can only imagine the joy that exploded in their hearts as they ran down the road to show the priests that they were now "clean." These must have been the happiest men who ever ran down that road. The curse was lifted. They could go home to family and friends. They would not hear any more jokes or ridicule. Self-respect and dignity were returned to them. They had been given a new life.

The Bible tells us that one of them, seeing that he was healed, came back praising God in a loud voice. Then he threw himself at Jesus' feet and thanked Him.

This Samaritan practiced an essential type of prayer. He said, "Thanks."

The saying "thanks" prayer is verbalizing the attitude of gratitude. It is expressing appreciation to God for His generosity. It is saying "Thank You" for the specific gifts He has given you. It is an indication of humility and the cure for complaining. And it is one of the most powerful things a person can do. Never underestimate the power of thanksgiving. It has the power to free God to do the impossible. Here is a story to illustrate that:

"You have to come right away!" the voice on the phone shouted in the middle of the night. "Diane's in the closet with a cord around her neck and says that she'll kill herself."

I crawled out of bed and got dressed. Diane and her family lived only a few minutes away and I was at their house before I was awake enough to do much other than pray. I gulped as I got out of the car and asked God to help me. I asked for wisdom and a miracle.

When I walked in, Diane was still in the closet and threatening suicide. Her husband Mark had lost his job. This new financial pressure, compounded by the presence of four tiny children, seemed like more than she could bear. All she saw ahead of her was hopelessness. She could not take it anymore and this was her desperate cry for help, an attempt to somehow relieve her despair.

That month I had been practicing saying "thanks" prayers in my personal times with God. As Mark and I walked up to the closet where Diane had barricaded herself, I felt a definite prompting from God to give her a proposition. I knew there was no way she could actually carry out the suicide before we could break down the door and rescue her, if it came to that. However, I was still shocked as these words came out of my mouth:

"Diane, I'll make you a deal. If we cannot come up with one hundred reasons for you to be thankful, you can go ahead and kill yourself. But if we come up with a hundred you have to come out and talk."

She cried out, "I am not thankful for anything. I just want to die."

"Not yet," I said. "Let us first at least try to come up with one hundred reasons to give thanks."

"Stacy, Katy, Lyndsey, and Matthew," her husband Mark said, naming their children. "That's four good reasons to be thankful."

"The fact that we live in a house and not an apartment. You said that just last week," he added anxiously. "That's five."

"Did you eat dinner tonight?" I asked. "Many people went to bed hungry tonight."

"Yes," she said.

"That's six!" Mark noted.

"How about having a car?" I asked.

"I am glad my grandma gave us that nice car," Diane whispered.

"That's seven, " Mark said.

"How about the cat?" I said, looking desperately around the house.

"I love that dumb cat," she said.

"Eight." I counted.

"What about your parents?" Mark asked. "They'd be nine and ten."

"And your brother and sister," he added.

"That's twelve," I said, keeping track.

"Plus your grandma makes thirteen," said Mark.

"And Grandpa," Diane said quietly.

"Fourteen," I said, smiling now. "Keep going."

Once she began to join in giving reasons to be thankful, the atmosphere in the house changed from despair to delight. We continued listing reasons to be thankful as the number mounted.

We began to list every piece of furniture in the house, and every article of food in the refrigerator. By the time we reached the number 50 we all were laughing. At number 75, Mark and I heard noises behind the door. The closet door creaked and Diane came out with a sheepish grin. "I am sorry to do this to you. I don't want to die. I have too much to live for," she said.

That is just one of the many experiences that taught me this important truth: Never underestimate the power of saying "thanks" to God. It frees God to do the impossible. It reminds us that we are too blessed to be depressed.

I wonder. Could it be that the heaviness that oppresses our souls would be lifted if we took more time to say "thanks"?

Don't you love the story of Jehoshaphat? (Aren't you glad your parents didn't name you Jehoshaphat?) He was the king of Judah when they were about to be invaded by three strong armies (see 2 Chron. 20:1). Judah had no hope against these powerhouse enemies. But Jehoshaphat believed in the power of thanksgiving. He appointed men to lead the way into battle by singing, "Give thanks to the Lord, for His love endures forever" (2 Chron. 20:21; see also Ps. 136:1).

Never underestimate the power of thanksgiving. It frees God to do the impossible—it certainly did for Jehoshaphat and Judah.

As they began to sing and praise, the Lord set ambushes against the men of Ammon and Moab and Mount Seir who were invading Judah, and they were defeated (2 Chronicles 20:22).

Saying "thanks" prayers freed God to do the impossible. The people of Judah did not even have to fight. Thanksgiving had opened the door for God to fight their enemies for them. Jehoshaphat's people only had to walk in and grab the spoils of victory.

Notice that it says, "As they began to sing and praise, the Lord set ambushes." The Lord set the ambushes as they gave thanks, not before. God did not act until they said "thanks."

I wonder. Could there be big, impossible things God wants to do in our lives that will not occur until we say "thanks"?

When Solomon was dedicating the temple, his heart was full of gratitude to the Lord. He also desperately wanted the Lord's presence to dwell there in a mighty way. In his lavish fashion, Solomon had all the Levites who were musicians gather on the east side of the altar with their cymbals, harps, and lyres. They were to be accompanied by 120 trumpet-playing priests and other singing priests. In unison they all joined together to praise and thank the Lord. They sang the same song Jehoshaphat's singers sang, "Give thanks to the Lord, for He is good. His love endures forever" (Ps. 136:1; see also 2 Chron. 5:13).

As they sang, a miracle occurred. The glory of the Lord filled the temple as a cloud (see 2 Chron. 5:13-14).

Wow! Never underestimate the power of saying "thanks" to God. It frees God to do the impossible. In this case it ushered in the glorious presence of God.

I wonder. Could it be that the glorious presence of God in our lives would be manifest if we took more time to say "thanks"? Could it be that the glorious presence of God we seek after will not be manifest until we say "thanks"?

Allow me to offer a few suggestions for applying the saying "thanks" prayer and experiencing the power of thanksgiving:

MAKE YOUR OWN THANKSGIVING LIST.

See if you can list 50—or even 100!—things for which you are grateful. Begin with spiritual blessings like the Bible, answered prayer, Heaven, forgiveness, the Holy Spirit, and your church. Try to list at least 10.

Now list some physical blessings like sight, the ability to walk, taste, and smell. Thank God for some of your material blessings, like clothes, food, a car, furniture, books, and so forth. Say "thanks" to God for meeting various financial needs.

Thank God for lessons He has been teaching you lately. Also thank Him regarding trials He has seen you through and how they have benefited your life. Thank God for things that you believe He is going to do for you in the future.

Say "thanks" to God for key people in your life. Think of family and friends, fellow workers and neighbors. Thank God for authorities and spiritual mentors. Conclude by giving thanks for pastors, teachers, and missionaries you know.

CULTIVATE THE ATTITUDE OF GRATITUDE.

For the next 24 hours or longer, make a conscious attempt to make certain that the only prayers you pray are saying "thanks" prayers. Turn every prayer into an expression of gratitude.

BE THANKFUL EVERY HOUR.

For the next few days, every time you notice the hour changing, say "thanks" to God for something. I had a friend who went so far as to set the alarm on his watch to go off every hour to remind him to give thanks. He said that within a week, it had wonderfully changed his attitude and walk with God.

God has some awesome blessings in store for you as you apply the saying "thanks" prayer. Never underestimate the power of thanksgiving.

Chapter 7

SETTING CAPTIVES FREE PRAYER

It had to be one of the worst single days any individual human ever experienced. Satan had sought and received permission to swallow Job up in a whirlwind of intense misery, and he did. In one dreadful day Job lost all seven sons and all three daughters; he lost all of his sheep, camels, oxen, and donkeys; and he lost all of his servants. In just a few hours his children, his business empire, his retirement holdings, and his career were all gone. Totally gone. Then, soon after that, his health was stolen and replaced with a rotting robe of agonizing boils. These awful events left his once-stainless reputation ruined and his heart broken.

Any hope of receiving encouragement from his friends quickly disappeared when they spoke. The only words they offered were words of rebuke and criticism. They dumped guilt and shame on him.

Poor Job became a captive in a prison of his pain and God's silence. He spent what must have felt like an eternity shackled in torment and shame.

Then one day it all turned around. Just as quickly as it came, bleak bondage was changed to abundant blessing. Job was released from grievous pain into glorious prosperity. The sun finally burst through the clouds and morning broke the darkness. God ended the captivity of Job. Boils disappeared and prosperity returned to Job. He ended up with twice as many sheep, camels, oxen, and donkeys as he had owned before. He had seven more sons and three more daughters. He was a prisoner set free.

But what made the difference? What was the key that turned the lock that opened the door of his jail cell? The answer is found in Job 42:10:

The Lord turned the captivity of Job, when he prayed for his friends: also the Lord gave Job twice as much as he had before (Job 42:10 KJV).

Notice the last six words, *"when he prayed for his friends."* Job prayed a "setting captives free prayer" and God did the rest.

The Lord had not been impressed by the self-righteous rebuke Job's friends brought to Job. They were in danger of judgment from the hand of God (see Job 42:7). How would they handle the level of adversity Job had faced?

But when Job prayed for them, God set Job free. Let me repeat that: When Job prayed for *them*, God set *Job* free! Earlier, when Job prayed for himself, his misery had not been removed. He remained stuck in a prison of pain and anguish. Almighty God was inactive and silent. But when Job prayed for others, the very ones who had hurt him and had compounded his misery, *then* God moved and set Job free!

When Job prayed for his tormenters, his own torment was removed. *After* he showed love for his enemies, God showed love to him. As he did something good to those who had misjudged him, God did good things for him. When he blessed those who cursed him, God blessed him. After he interceded for those who had mistreated him, God treated him to a banquet of freedom and fulfillment.

The power of setting captives free is that when we set others free, it releases God to set us free.

⸻◉⸻

"Setting captives free prayer" is prayer offered on behalf of "enemies." It is a higher expression of love as you "do good to those who hate you, bless those who curse you, [and] pray for those who mistreat you" (Luke 6:27-28). It is releasing others from the debt of hurt they caused you and seeing your soul released from the prison cell of bitterness. It is praying for your tormentors in such a way that releases you from your own torment and places you in the flow of God's greater blessings. It is saying with Jesus, "Father, forgive them, for they do not know what they are doing" (Luke 23:34).

Jesus described "setting captives free prayer" in the Sermon on the Mount when He said, "But I tell you who hear Me: Love your enemies, do good to those who hate you, bless those who curse you, pray for those who mistreat you" (Luke 6:27-28).

I confess that I struggle with "setting captives free prayer." It is impossible to do in the flesh. When I am mistreated, I want to fight back. I want revenge. When I am cursed I want to curse back. When hated, I fight the hatred that wells up from my heart.

The only prayers I want to pray when I am hurt are imprecatory prayers of "God break their teeth and give them a bad case of diarrhea." I want to pray the Irish prayer: "Lord, as for my enemies, please turn their hearts. If not, please turn their ankles so I'll know them by their limp."

But bitterness is a jail cell. It chains us to our enemies and makes us their prisoner. Jesus said the only way out is through forgiveness. And Job showed that it is expressed in prayer.

The last two years I seem to have been given an unprecedented number of chances to practice "setting captives free prayer." There have been hurts against myself, offenses to my church, and wrongs done to my family. I have been blindsided by soul-piercing arrows fired by close friends and heart-crushing hand grenades tossed by total strangers. I have sensed bitterness trying to take root and a desire for vengeance attempting to shackle my soul.

Thank God for the "setting captives free prayer"! The power of setting captives free is that as we set others free it releases God to set us free. As I have prayed for my "enemies," I have been set free.

———— ⊰⦿⊱ ————

Jesus taught us about the power of setting captives free in Matthew 18:23-35. He tells of a man whose king forgave him for a debt that could be described as nearly limitless. His debt was equal to the total amount of taxes Rome collected from four provinces over an 11-year period![1] This could be called a multi-billion-dollar debt.

Yet, right after experiencing the king's extreme mercy, the fabulously forgiven man refused to forgive the debt that another man owed him, even though it was much smaller. That man's debt could be called a several-thousand-dollar debt.[2] Instead of forgiving his debtor, the forgiven man threw his debtor into prison.

When the forgiven man's king found out what he had done, he had him thrown into jail and tortured. The forgiven man's refusal to forgive led to his own imprisonment.

This parable teaches us several necessary truths:

1. God, just as the king in the story, has forgiven us a massive debt that is greater than we could ever repay.

2. We, just as the man in the story, should forgive others of the comparably smaller debts they owe us (a few thousand dollars compared to several billion dollars).

3. Appreciating the great amount of debt from which God has forgiven us should motivate us to forgive others.

4. Failing to forgive others places us in captivity.

———≈◉≈———

Jesus faced His greatest hour of need. Judas betrayed Him. His closest friends deserted Him. Peter denied Him, and others fled for their lives.

Jesus had given over three years of His life to loving, teaching, healing, and feeding people. Yet those same people cried out for His death with the brutal words, "Crucify Him! Crucify Him!"

The Jewish leaders plotted His death, Pilate ordered it, and the Romans carried it out. They beat Him, spit on Him, and drove a crown of thorns into His head. They spiked His hands and feet to cross pieces of wood and hung Him up before a jeering crowd. He had to fight for every breath in agony against the spikes. The thief beside Him mocked and scorned Him.

All of these people had hurt Him. But Jesus did not bow to bitterness. He refused to take His revenge. His hands and feet were bound, but not His soul. He resisted the massive inner urge to let bitterness take His soul captive. Instead He prayed a "setting captives free prayer" when He said, "Father, forgive them, for they do not know what they are doing" (Luke 23:34).

———◦◦◦———

It is not a fun assignment but it is very valuable. Every month I make a list. I ask God to show me anyone against whom I am holding a grudge. This happens to be one of those prayers God always answers right away. I am always surprised at the length of this list as the Holy Spirit brings names and faces to mind that I had consciously put out of my mind. Embarrassed, I realize that the hurts, real or perceived, that I felt because of these people have at some level held me captive. I ask God to forgive them of any wrong they may have done to me. I also choose to forgive them. I consciously release them from any debt they owe me. Then I pray for God to bless them in the same ways I want Him to bless me.

Every time I work through this painful practice of releasing my debtors, God sets me free. I find that I am closer to Him when I have forgiven them. He hears my prayers for my needs as I have prayed for their needs.

Let me encourage you to pray for those who have hurt you. It is one of the simplest, most important and powerful types of prayer you can pray because as we set others free, it releases God to set us free.

ENDNOTES

1. John MacArthur, *The MacArthur New Testament Commentary: Matthew 16-23* (Chicago, IL: Moody Press, 1988), p. 148.
2. John Bevere, *The Bait of Satan* (Lake Mary, FL: Charisma House, 1994), p. 135.

Chapter 8

SPREAD IT OUT BEFORE THE LORD PRAYER

Poor guy. The hair on his neck must have stood on end. His stomach must have turned in knots. Hezekiah, king of Judah, faced his worst fear: Sennacherib, the undefeated king of Assyria. Sennacherib had a huge army and, in the literal sense, cutting-edge chariots. He had destroyed all of the nations around Judah, from Lebanon in the north to Egypt in the south. And now he was ready to ride his mighty war chariots to victory right through Judah.

In order to intimidate Hezekiah, Sennacherib sent a message reminding them of his complete destruction of nine city-states that had already opposed him. He wanted them to make no mistake; he intended to make Judah number ten, unless they surrendered to become slaves taken captive back to Assyria.

For Hezekiah the stress must have been unbearable. He was in between a rock and a boulder. Option A: Watch your nation get crushed by a superior force and under the wheels of thundering chariots? Or Option B: See your people shackled and led away to Assyria to be slaves? What could he do?

Hezekiah chose Option C. He did what we all should do when we face extreme pressure and ferocious enemy attacks.

Hezekiah received the letter from the messengers and read it. Then he went up to the temple of the Lord and spread it out before the Lord (2 Kings 19:14).

Notice carefully the last six words of verse 14: "spread it out before the Lord." He took Sennacherib's letter and went up to the temple of the Lord. There he spread it out before the Lord in prayer.

Option C was a great idea. Look at what happened:

That night the angel of the Lord went out and put to death a hundred and eighty-five thousand men in the Assyrian camp. When the people got up the next morning—there were all the dead bodies! (2 Kings 19:35)

Spreading his problems out before the Lord in prayer was the smart choice! That night the angel of the Lord went out and killed 185,000 men in the Assyrian camp. When Sennacherib woke up and saw what had happened, he was so shook up that he and his army packed up and marched straight home. God did not like Sennacherib's arrogance, but He did like Hezekiah's prayer.

All King Hezekiah's soldiers had to do was collect the booty that the Assyrians had left behind in their hasty retreat. Hezekiah had turned the problem over to God; God fought their battle; and God won.

———◈———

"Spread it out before the Lord prayer" is spreading your problems out before the Lord and letting Him sort them out. It is replacing worry with prayer. It is turning every pressure and problem into prayer. It is making your worry list into your prayer list. It is refusing to worry because you are choosing to pray. It is casting all of your cares on Him because He cares for you.

Paul taught it and encouraged us to practice "spread it out before the Lord prayer" when he wrote:

Do not be anxious about anything, but in everything, by prayer and petition, with thanksgiving, present your requests to God. And the peace of God, which transcends all understanding, will guard your hearts and your minds in Christ Jesus (Philippians 4:6-7).

Peter advocated "spread it out before the Lord prayer" when he wrote, "Cast all your anxiety on Him because He cares for you" (1 Pet. 5:7).

It is a privilege to possess several spiritual gifts. But I have to confess that I also possess the non-spiritual gift of anxiety. I am highly analytical and when I cannot figure out how something will work out I struggle to find peace with it. Unresolved situations and uncertain circumstances drive me to distraction. Therefore, I am eternally grateful for "spread it out before the Lord prayer."

I have learned that in order to keep from being eaten by anxiety, I must spread it out before the Lord in prayer. Every morning I take whatever I am worried about and write it down in my prayer journal. The list usually has four to eight worries listed. (One day it had 57!) This is how I spread it out before the Lord. I take each item on my list and give it to God. I turn my pressure list into my prayer list. One by one, I cast all my cares on Him. By doing this I replace worry with prayer.

When I do this, simple yet wonderful things happen. My pressure turns to peace. My concerns turn into confidence. My burdens are lifted. My head is lifted. I feel better.

As Paul said, "The peace of God, which transcends all understanding, guards our hearts and minds in Christ Jesus" (see Phil. 4:7). Peace replaces pressure and anxiety. When we give our problems to the God who is greater than our problems, we have a peace that is greater than our problems. When we fail to experience such peace, could it be that we have failed to really give our problems to God in prayer?

But, the beauty of prayer is more than how it makes us feel. The beauty of prayer is what it does. It invites God into the situation. It turns the problem over to the One who is big enough to handle it. And He does.

I generally like to go back at night or the next morning and look back over my prayer list. I need to do this because by evening I often forget what I was worried about in the morning. God has already worked it out. I love to put checks by all answered prayers. And there are many answered prayers. Some of my concerns never materialized. Some did and God defeated them that day. In other areas of concern, I did not see the full answer, but I did see God working.

Are you facing some difficult decisions, anxious situations, or tough adversaries? Then you are a candidate for "spread it out before the Lord prayer." Go to your place of prayer. Write down your worries. Spread them out before the Lord. Ask Him to take care of them. Then leave them with Him and go off into victory.

Chapter 9

SEARCHING PRAYER

Earlier this year my father-in-law visited us. He looked very good for a 72-year-old man. He thought he might have a cold because he had a small yet persistent cough. But no one thought much of it. Then, in mid-October, we got a call telling us that my father-in-law had suffered a stroke. The doctors took X-rays and discovered that he had several blocked arteries and needed an operation. When they opened him up they found that they could not complete the surgery they had planned because his heart was blocked by a cancerous tumor, and he also had cancer in his lungs. No one would have known that he had cancer if they had not opened up his chest for surgery.

The Bible clearly states that we live on a sin-cursed planet and that all of us have a sin nature. Because of the sin in our world and the nature of our hearts, it is easy for our hearts to develop potentially dangerous spiritual diseases. Bitterness may take root and eat us up like cancer. Selfishness and pride can create blockages that keep the life of God from flowing through us. Rebellion, anxiety, fear, greed, envy, lust, and worldliness are other devastating "heart diseases."

King David was a man after God's own heart, but later in life he learned that he could not trust his own heart. He knew from painful failure that even though things may appear healthy on the outside, there could be disease within. So David offered a prayer, a searching prayer, asking God to look in, to X-ray, to open up his chest and examine his heart:

Search me, O God, and know my heart; test me and know my anxious thoughts. See if there is any offensive way in me, and lead me in the way everlasting (Psalm 139:23-24).

Searching prayer is inviting the Lord to search your heart to its depths. It is opening up to the scrutiny of the "Heart Surgeon." It is asking God to see into our inner being and show us what is truly in our hearts that we might be cleansed, healed, liberated, comforted, and changed. It is not a journey into ourselves, but a journey *through* ourselves to emerge *from* self and more deeply into God.

I wonder. Have you ever had the courage to invite God to examine your heart? How long has it been since you had the courage to allow God to perform heart surgery? When was the last time you asked God to reveal where bitterness has taken root, or where selfishness and pride have begun to block the life of God from flowing through you? When was the last time you were willing to ask God to search your heart of rebellion, anxiety, fear, greed, envy, lust, and worldliness?

Several times a year I take some time away from people to get alone with God and allow Him to search my heart. Often I go through a list to make me look in areas I am naturally reluctant to search. Below is one of the lists I have found helpful on many occasions. It is fairly thorough and can be highly convicting. Let me encourage you to read slowly through this list, asking the Holy Spirit to search your heart for potentially cancerous sins.

1. *Matthew 6:12-15*—Is there anyone against whom you hold a grudge? Anyone you haven't forgiven? Anyone you hate? Anyone you do not love? Are there any misunderstandings that you are unwilling to forget? Is there any person against whom you harbor bitterness, resentment, or jealousy? Anyone you dislike to hear praised or well spoken of? Do you allow anything to justify a wrong attitude toward another?

2. *Matthew 6:33*—Where do you struggle to put God first? Are your decisions made according to your own desires and wisdom, rather than seeking and following God's will? Do any of the following, in any way, interfere with your surrender and service to God: ambition, pleasures, loved ones, friendships, desire for recognition, money, hobbies, a career, comfort and convenience, or your plans?

3. *Mark 16:15*—Have you grown cold in your concern to seek the lost for Christ? Have you failed to witness with your mouth for the Lord Jesus Christ? Have you been lax in praying for the lost?

4. *John 13:35*—Are you secretly pleased over the misfortune of others? Are you secretly annoyed over the accomplishments or advancements of another? Are you guilty of contention or strife? Do you quarrel, argue, or engage in heated discussions? Are you a partaker of any divisions? Are there people whom you deliberately slight?

5. *Acts 20:35*—Have you robbed God by withholding His due time, talents, and money? Have you failed to support mission work either in prayer or in offerings?

6. *1 Corinthians 4:2*—Are there areas where you are so undependable that you cannot be trusted with responsibilities in the Lord's work? Are you allowing your emotions to be stirred for things of the Lord, but doing nothing about it?

7. *1 Corinthians 10:31*—Do you take the credit for the good about you, rather than give all the glory to God? Do you talk of what you have done rather than of what Christ has done? Are your thoughts or statements mostly about "I," "me," and "mine"? Are your feelings easily hurt? Have you made a pretense of being something that you are not?

8. *Ephesians 3:20*—Are you self-conscious rather than Christ-conscious? Do you allow feelings of inferiority to keep you from attempting things you should in serving God?

9. *Ephesians 4:28*—Do you do a minimum level of work? Have you been careless in the payment of your debts? Have you sought to evade payment of debts? Do you waste time? Do you waste the time of others?

10. *Ephesians 4:31*—Do you complain? Do you find fault? Do you have critical attitudes toward any person or thing? Are you irritable or cranky?

Do you ever carry hidden anger? Do you get angry? Do you become impatient with others? Are you ever harsh or unkind?

11. *Ephesians 5:15-16*—Do you listen to un-edifying music, watch ungodly things, or read unworthy books or magazines? Do you find it necessary to seek satisfaction from a questionable source? Are you doing certain things that show you are not satisfied in the Lord Jesus Christ?

12. *Ephesians 5:20*—Have you neglected to thank Him for all things (the seemingly bad as well as the good)? Have you virtually called God a liar by doubting His Word? Do you worry? Is your spiritual temperature based on your feelings instead of on the facts of God's Word?

13. *Philippians 1:21*—Are you taken up with the cares of this life? Do you derive your joy from things or circumstances rather than from the Lord and His Word? Does something else mean more to you than living for and pleasing Christ?

14. *Philippians 2:4*—Do you ever, by word or deed, seek to hurt someone? Do you gossip? Do you speak unkindly concerning people when they are not present? Do you carry prejudice against true Christians because they are of some different group than yours, or because they do not see everything exactly like you do?

15. *Philippians 4:4*—Do you carry any bitterness toward God? Have you complained against Him in any way? Have you been dissatisfied with His provision for you? Is there in your heart any unwillingness to obey God fully? Do you have any reservations as to what you would not do concerning anything that might be His will? Have you disobeyed some direct leading from Him?

16. *Colossians 3:9*—Do you engage in empty and unprofitable conversation? Do you ever lie? Do you ever exaggerate? Cheat? Steal? Over-charge?

17. *2 Timothy 2:22*—Do you allow impure thoughts about the opposite sex to stay in your mind? Do you read that which is impure or suggests unholy things? Do you indulge in entertainment that is unclean? Are you guilty of the lustful look?[1]

After answering these questions, confess your sins. Accept forgiveness. Thank God for the blood of Jesus that cleanses us from all unrighteousness. And read the next chapter on "sorrow over sin prayer."

ENDNOTES

1. Harold Vaughan, Adapted from the pamphlet, *Heart Searching for Prayer, Preparation, and Personal Revival* (Vinton, VA: Christ Life Publications, 1985)

Chapter 10

SORROW OVER SIN PRAYER

You know the story. David was in his midlife crisis time. He had worked hard to climb the ladder of success and had let down his defenses. He had risen to the point where he did not think he needed to be accountable to anyone or obey the same rules everyone else did. This was a dangerous place to be.

Arrogance and lust stormed his heart and took root. Eventually the lust overpowered his heart and he committed adultery with Bathsheba. His pride got the upper hand and he tried to cover his sin by having Bathsheba's husband killed. Then he tried to deny his sin. His resulting guilt and shame grew stronger every day. He found himself swallowed up in the misery of unresolved sin.

Later he recalled that draining, dreadful, painful period with these words:

When I kept silent, my bones wasted away through my groaning all day long. For day and night Your hand was heavy upon me; my strength was sapped as in the heat of summer (Psalm 32:3-4).

Finally out of His mercy and grace, God sent a prophet named Nathan to confront David about his sins. David reviewed that defining moment in what we know as Psalm 51, which has this caption: "A psalm of David. When the prophet Nathan came to him after David had committed adultery with Bathsheba."

Have mercy on me, O God, according to Your unfailing love; according to Your great compassion blot out my transgressions. Wash away all my iniquity and cleanse me from my sin. For I know my transgressions, and my sin is always before me. Against You, You only, have I sinned and done what is evil in Your sight, so that You are proved right when You speak and justified when You judge. Surely I was sinful at birth, sinful from the time my mother conceived me. Surely You desire truth in the inner parts; You teach me wisdom in the inmost place. Cleanse me with hyssop, and I will be clean; wash me, and I will be whiter than snow. Let me hear joy and gladness; let the bones you have crushed rejoice. Hide Your face from my sins and blot out all my iniquity. Create in me a pure heart, O God, and renew a steadfast spirit within me (Psalm 51:1-10).

This psalm is a great example of "sorrow over sin prayer." It shows us that it is not enough to let the Lord examine our hearts and show us our sin; we must take the next step and let our sorrow over that sin lead us to confess it.

David was sorry for his sin and meant business with God about being cleansed of it. Look back at Psalm 51. Notice the way David heaped up a multitude of requests as he confessed his sin: "Have mercy on me…blot out my transgressions. Wash away all my iniquity and cleanse me from my sin…Cleanse me with hyssop…wash me…Hide Your face from my sins and blot out all my iniquity."

Such serious sorrow over sin does not go without reward. It ushers in a host of wonderful blessings:

1. *Renewed joy*— "Let me hear joy and gladness; let the bones You have crushed rejoice.… Restore to me the joy of Your salvation" (Ps. 51:8,12).

2. *Rekindled passion*— "Create in me a pure heart, O God, and renew a steadfast spirit within me. …Grant me a willing spirit, to sustain me" (Ps. 51:10,12).

3. *Restored confidence*— "Then I will teach transgressors Your ways, and sinners will turn back to You" (Ps. 51:13).

4. *Refreshed song*— "Save me from bloodguilt, O God, the God who saves me, and my tongue will sing of Your righteousness. O Lord, open my lips, and my mouth will declare Your praise" (Ps. 51:14-15).

"Sorrow over sin prayer" is letting the sin in our hearts break our hearts. It is seeing sin as God sees it. It is letting the pain that our sin caused the Father and Jesus on the cross fill our thoughts, stir our emotions, and change our wills. It is saying the same thing about our sins that God says.

It is not enough to let the Lord examine our hearts and show us our sin. We must take the next step and let our sorrow over that sin lead us to confess it—not excuse it, rationalize it, or blame it on someone else.

If we confess our sins, He is faithful and just and will forgive us our sins and purify us from all unrighteousness (1 John 1:9).

The word *confess* means to say the same thing, which basically means that we say the same thing about our sin that God says. It is not a mistake, a mess-up, an error, or misbehavior. It is sin. It is wrong. It must be forgiven. It needs to be washed off our record and purified from our hearts.

He who conceals his sins does not prosper, but whoever confesses and renounces them finds mercy (Proverbs 28:13).

There is a powerful truth revealed in Proverbs 28:13: *Sin is unconquered until it is uncovered.* "Sorrow over sin prayer" is refusing to cover your sin before God. It is uncovering your sin and confessing it so that God may grant you mercy and give you victory over it.

What sin do you need to uncover before God? What sin do you need to confess to God today? Do you need to ask for forgiveness? Do you need to be washed and purified? Do you need to practice "sorrow over sin prayer"?

Chapter 11

SINGING PRAISES PRAYER

What do you do when your situation is miserable with little or no hope of relief? What *should* you do? Paul and Silas faced such a predicament after arriving in Philippi hoping to plant a church. Instead, they found themselves in prison. They had cast a demon out of a fortune-telling slave girl. However, the girl's owners did not appreciate the potential lost income, so they stirred up the crowd and the authorities against Paul and Silas. As a result the missionaries were severely beaten and taken to the inner cell of the prison where their feet were locked in stocks.

I don't know what you would do, but I have a tendency toward self-pity. Such a rotten time would lead me to pout and whine—but not Paul and Silas. They refused the urge to pout and whine, and instead they embraced praise and worship. The Bible says it this way:

About midnight Paul and Silas were praying and singing hymns to God, and the other prisoners were listening to them (Acts 16:25).

We do not know what hymns they sang to God, although one of the most popular lyrics in the Psalms is found in Psalm 118. When you see how appropriate the words of this Psalm are to their plight, it is easy to imagine them regaling God and the other prisoners with this song.

Give thanks to the Lord, for He is good; His love endures forever....In my anguish I cried to the Lord, and He answered by setting me free. The Lord is with me; I will not be afraid. What can man do to me? The Lord is with me; He is my helper. I will look in triumph on my enemies. It is better to take refuge in the Lord than to trust in man. It is better to take refuge in the Lord than to trust in princes.... The Lord is my strength and my song; He has become my salvation.... I will not die but live, and will proclaim what the Lord has done.... This is the day the Lord has made; let us rejoice and be glad in it. O Lord, save us; O Lord, grant us success.... You are my God, and I will give You thanks; You are my God, and I will exalt You. Give thanks to the Lord, for He is good; His love endures forever (Psalm 118).

God obviously heard and enjoyed their singing prayer of praise and worship. Instead of leaving them in their awful state, He acted on their behalf in a big way.

Suddenly there was such a violent earthquake that the foundations of the prison were shaken. At once all the prison doors flew open, and everybody's chains came loose (Acts 16:26).

Wow! (Say it backward: Wow!) They had a praise quake and God sent an earthquake. (I imagine the song the other prisoners started singing was, "There's a whole lotta' shakin' going on.") Paul and Silas magnified God and God moved on their behalf. But that's not all.

The jailer woke up... (Acts 16:27).

They had a praise quake, God sent an earthquake, and the jailer got awake. But that's not all...

...and when he saw the prison doors open, he drew his sword and was about to kill himself because he thought the prisoners had escaped. But Paul shouted, "Don't harm yourself! We are all here!" The jailer called for lights, rushed in and fell trembling before Paul and Silas. He then brought them out and asked, "Sirs, what must I do to be saved?" (Acts 16:27-30)

They had a praise quake, God sent an earthquake, and the jailer got awake and began to shake. But that's not all...

They replied, "Believe in the Lord Jesus, and you will be saved—you and your household." Then they spoke the word of the Lord to him and to all the others in his house. At that hour of the night the jailer took them and washed their wounds; then immediately he and all his family were baptized (Acts 16:31-33).

They had a praise quake, God sent an earthquake, the jailer got awake and began to shake. Then he and his family got saved for Heaven's sake! Wow! (Say it backward: Wow!)

Because of Paul and Silas' singing prayer of praise and worship two miracles occurred: ground-shaking convulsions and Heaven-making conversions! Never underestimate the power of "singing praises prayer."

⸻

"Singing praises prayer" is singing to the Lord in psalms, hymns, and spiritual songs. It is making your own psalter of love songs to the Lord. It is letting your love for the Lord flow out in melody. It is singing *to* the Lord and not just *about* the Lord. It is fulfilling your priestly duties. It is practicing the serious business of Heaven.

Several years ago my good friend Jack lost his teenage son in an apparent suicide. Jack did not know or have any definite way of knowing the spiritual state of the boy at his death. Obviously this was a crushing loss. What do you do in such a dire situation? What should you do?

When Jack went to the grave, the Holy Spirit stirred something deep within Jack's soul. He is not a singer, but he is a God-lover. Before he knew what was happening a song of praise was in his head, his heart, and on his lips.

On the long drive back from the cemetery he turned on praise music in his car and sang along as the tears rolled down his cheeks. Later he told me, "Dave, praise is the thing that has sustained me."

⸻

I do not know your circumstances, but I do know this: Anytime is an appropriate time to praise the Lord. Any place is an appropriate place to praise the Lord. Any occasion is an appropriate occasion to praise the Lord. Why not lift your favorite praise song to the Lord right now? It certainly cannot hurt anything, and it might just open the door to miracles.

Chapter 12

"Selfish" Prayer

I was completely, totally, absolutely broke. As a sophomore at a Christian college, I had spent my summer as a missionary in England instead of working a summer job. As a result I had no money for anything other than my tuition, books, and room and board.

I also had a problem. I needed a haircut or I would be in violation of the school hair code. My Resident Assistant, an ex-Marine who thought a dorm ought to run like boot camp, gave me 24 hours to get it cut, or else. I looked at the dismal prospects of having no hope for getting a decent haircut for free, as all of my friends were notorious butchers with a pair of scissors.

That night I read about the man in Luke 11 who went to his friend and asked him to give him three loaves of bread. "Then He said to them, 'Suppose one of you has a friend, and he goes to him at midnight and says, "Friend, lend me three loaves of bread" ' " (Luke 11:5).

I was struck with the seemingly selfish nature of his request, "Lend me three loaves." I had always been a bit tentative to pray such selfish sounding prayers. But I needed a haircut or I would be disciplined.

As I read on in that passage I was impressed with the promise Jesus made in verse 9. He seemed to be saying that it was all right to boldly ask for what you need: "So I say to you: Ask and it will be given to you; seek and you will find; knock and the door will be opened to you" (Luke 11:9).

I also thought of the promise made in James 4:2-3: "You do not have, because you do not ask God. When you ask, you do not receive, because you ask with wrong motives, that you may spend what you get on your pleasures."

I knew my motives were unselfish and my need was real. So, rather sheepishly, I told God that I desired three loaves: (1) A good haircut, (2) within 24 hours, (3) for free. When I stated those "selfish" things I hoped I would not be struck by lightning. But as I prayed I felt the apprehension swept away by a wonderful sense of peace and boldness before the throne of grace. In minutes I dosed off to sleep.

The next day I forgot all about my need of a haircut. But I am glad God did not. At the dinner table a friend introduced me to a girl who was new to our college. As we talked, she said that she had graduated from beauty school and her dad had made her attend a Christian college for a semester. She said that she really missed cutting hair and was thinking of starting a haircutting business on the side. Then she looked at me and said, "You have a nice head of hair. You know, I miss haircutting so much, I would cut yours free."

Later that evening I had to smile as I sat in a chair listening to her whistle and watching the hair drop around my feet. God had heard my simple, specific prayer. He had given me my three loaves: a good haircut, in less than 24 hours, for free!

Selfish prayer is asking God to bless you as only God can bless you. It is the prayer of "me"—"bless me," "help me," "give me," "lead me." It is praying the personal prayers of the Old Testament.

Several years ago as I read through the Bible I prayed every prayer prayed in the Bible. I figured, if it worked for them it can work for me. I discovered that there are several awesome "selfish" prayers in the Bible, especially in the Old Testament. These include:

1. The Servant Prayer: "Give me success today" (Gen. 24:12).

2. The Jacob Prayer: "Bless me" (Gen. 32:26).

3. The Moses Prayer: "Teach me Your ways" (Exod. 33:13).

4. The Gideon Prayer: "Give me a sign" (Judg. 6:17).

5. The Hannah Prayer: "Remember me" (1 Sam. 1:11).

6. The Samuel Prayer: "Speak, [to me] Lord" (1 Sam. 3:10).

7. The David Prayer: "Cleanse me" (Ps. 51:17).

8. The Jabez Prayer: "Bless me, enlarge my territory, be with me, and keep me from harm" (1 Chron. 4:10).

9. The Solomon Prayer: "Give me wisdom to lead Your people" (2 Chron. 1:10).

10. The Nehemiah Prayer: "Strengthen my hands" (Neh. 6:9).

11. The Isaiah Prayer: "Send me" (Is. 6:8).

These prayers are very personal and in some cases almost sound "selfish"— "Give *me*," "Bless *me*," "Teach *me*," "Remember *me*." As I first began to pray the prayers I sometimes wondered, is this all right? Should I really be doing this? Will I get in trouble with God? But I reasoned, if these prayers were wrong, why would God answer them positively and then record them for us to read? Now I figure that if these prayers were good enough for God to answer *then*, they are good enough for me to ask *now*.

Sometimes we think that it is wrong to pray for ourselves. I remember telling a business friend of mine to pray the Servant Prayer, "Give me success today." He blushed and said that he thought it would be wrong for him to pray such a "selfish" prayer.

I told him that Abraham's servant did it and God answered him. Nehemiah did it and God answered him. I do it and God answers me. So he tried and found that God not only answered "selfish" prayers when offered by a servant, Nehemiah, or Dave, but when he prayed them as well. Now he's sold on "selfish" prayers.

The idea of praying selfish sounding prayers is addressed by a great man of prayer:

"What shall we ask for when we pray? That is answered many times in the Bible. We are to ask for everything we want. Anything that you have a right to want, you have a right to ask for. Every Christian should take every desire to God in prayer. It is a sin to want something you cannot honestly pray for, and you should ask God to remove the desire if it is wrong. And if the desire is not wrong, then you ought to ask God to fulfill it."[1]

God has even more in store for you than you can possibly imagine. We need to learn the life-changing adventure of praying "selfish" prayers. We need to learn to ask God for what we want or quit wanting it.

Endnotes

1. John R. Rice, *Prayer: Asking and Receiving* (Chicago, IL: Moody Press, 1961), p. 130.

Part 3
Difference-Making Prayers

Chapter 13

SELFLESS PRAYER

Delores McFarland was dying with congestive heart failure. Her heart was so weak that her kidneys and other vital organs were starting to shut down because her heart was not able to supply them. The doctor told the family to get prepared because there was no hope.

They asked our Pastoral Care Pastor, Scott, to meet with them to pray. He gathered the family (about 15 people) in a circle and asked them what they wanted him to pray for. They said, "Ask for a miracle." So he did.

Scott and others from New Life went down to visit Delores several times that week to pray with her. Several of our small groups prayed for God to do a miracle in Delores's life. Delores's newly Christian daughters continued to pray for God to heal their mom. They gave her cards with Scriptures and the message of the gospel.

Soon God did the first miracle as both Delores and her husband, Romi, confirmed their faith in Christ as Savior. The doctor's prognosis remained the same. He said that it was just a matter of time. They could not stop the bleeding and had to continue to give her a unit of blood daily. Yet, after that first prayer meeting, her spirits seemed to be getting better and she said she was starting to feel stronger. Scott began to believe that God was indeed doing a miracle.

The doctors set a date to send her home to die. Yet, when they gave her the final check before releasing her, they were shocked. They were amazed to find that her platelet counts were increasing from 10,000 to over 142,000 without blood transfusions. She soon went home, came to church, got baptized, and is doing great over a year later! The doctor said that he was not a religious man but believed he had seen a miracle.

Wow! The prayers of a few people made a big difference. People are now saved who were lost. A lady is alive who was supposed to be dead. Many learned the power of selfless intercessory prayer.

And now for the rest of the story…

For quite a while Scott had a painful ringing in his ears. It grew steadily worse until he went to the doctor. After several tests he was stunned to learn that he had a tumor growing on the stem of his brain. It could be removed but he could lose control of the muscles in his face or could be paralyzed or even die during the surgery.

Delores and her family, along with hundreds of others who had been blessed by Scott's calls and hospital visits, prayed for him. They prayed for him as he had prayed for them. They asked for God's will and a miracle.

Scott came through the surgery with flying colors. He has full control of the muscles in his face. Instead of being flat on his back for two weeks, he was up and around in record time. He even came to church a few days later so people could see the answer to their prayers. His surgeon, a non-believer, told him the success of the surgery had to be attributed to "Someone up there," pointing toward the heavens. We know that the "Someone" the doctor referred to is the Lord God who loves to answer selfless prayers.

And now for the rest of that story…

Derek was newly saved. He was struggling with addiction to alcohol, among other things. His first Sunday at our church was the one where we prayed for God to do a miracle and bring Scott through brain surgery successfully. Derek was touched by the prayers for Scott and prayed diligently for Scott all week. The next Sunday he was stunned to see Scott walk into church and worship God. Seeing what God did for Scott confirmed to Derek that God would set him free from his addictions. And God did!

$$\sim\!\!\Longrightarrow\!\!\bullet((\bullet))\!\!\Longleftarrow\!\!\sim$$

Selfless prayer is our way of loving others by asking God to meet their needs. It is asking God to bless others in the same ways we desire Him to bless us.

Dick Eastman helps us understand the essence and importance of selfless or intercessory prayer when he writes:

"Basically intercession is prayer offered on behalf of another. When the prayer warrior intercedes he forgets his personal needs and focuses all of his faith and prayer-attention on others. …The ministry of intercession, that of earnestly appealing on behalf of another, is especially important because it is the believer's common ground for Christian service. Spiritually speaking prayer is the divine equalizer. Some preach, others teach, a few sing publicly, but all can pray."[1]

Praying for others is the type of prayer God loves to respond to and answer. For example, a study was done in which 130 pastors, evangelists, and missionaries were prayed for by 130 trained intercessors for 15 minutes every day for a year.

About 89 percent of those surveyed indicated that the prayer had caused a positive change in their ministry. They reported more effectiveness in the use of their various gifts, a higher level of positive response to their ministry, more discernment and wisdom from God, increased wholeness and completeness in Christ, improved attitudes, more evidence of the fruit of the Spirit, better personal prayer lives, and heightened leadership skills.

The survey found that daily prayer for the leaders was more effective than weekly or monthly prayer. Also it was discovered that the prayers seemed to take a few weeks to begin to have an effect.[2]

In another study, researchers at Columbia University reported that women at an in vitro fertilization clinic in South Korea had a higher pregnancy rate when, unknown to the patients, strangers were asked to pray for their success. Women who were prayed for became pregnant twice as often as those who did not have people praying for them. The lead author of the report published in the *Journal of Reproductive Health*, Dr. Rogerio A. Lobo, Columbia's chairman of obstetrics and gynecology, was initially reluctant to publish the findings. But the differing pregnancy rates of the two groups of women proved to be too significant to ignore. "It was not even something that was borderline significant. It was highly significant."[3]

Yet, another study revealed that AIDS patients who were prayed for an hour a day, six days a week for 10 weeks were significantly healthier than those who received no prayer. During the six-month study, patients who were prayed for required 85 percent fewer days of hospitalization and 29 percent fewer doctor visits, and developed 83 percent fewer new illnesses than the control group.[4]

Not only is it effective when we selflessly pray for others, I believe it blesses us as well. The Bible teaches the principle of sowing and reaping (see Gal. 6:7). The principle of sowing and reaping applies in all areas of life, including prayer. When we ask God to bless someone else's marriage, He not only blesses *their* marriage, He blesses *our* marriage. When we ask God to bless someone else's finances, He not only blesses *their* finances, He blesses *ours*. When we ask God to bless someone else's ministry, he blesses ours. When we ask God to bless someone else's health, He is more likely to bless ours.

Let me encourage you to spend all of your prayer time today praying for the needs of others. Take a vacation from your needs and focus your faith and prayer-attention on the needs of others. Pray for them with as much determination and passion as you would want someone else praying for you.

Endnotes

1. Dick Eastman, *The Hour That Changes the World* (Grand Rapids, MI: Baker Book House, 1978), p. 76-77.
2. Peter Wagner, *Prayer Shield* (Ventura, CA: Regal Books, 1992), p. 74.
3. As quoted in an article by Monique I. Cuvelier, "Can Prayer Get You Pregnant?" *Psychology Today*, Jan-Feb 2002.
4. Katherine Gallia, Susanne Althoff, and Melissa Nachatelo, "Power of Prayer," *Natural Health*, April 1999.

Chapter 14

"Send Me" Prayer

I woke up that day just like every other day. I read a few chapters of my Bible and briefly prayed about the day. The only thing out of the ordinary was that I did something I had done on only a few other occasions. I happened to specifically pray a "send me" prayer. I told God to send me to make a difference in someone's life for His sake. Then I forgot about it and went off to work.

All morning long I had a gnawing thought. "I need a haircut. I ought to go to the mall and get it." I am a thrifty (some might even say "cheap") person. I had never gone to the salon in the mall for a haircut before. I usually saved money by having some student on campus do it for a few bucks. But over and over I kept getting the thought that I needed to go to the mall for a haircut.

Just before lunch I remembered that I had prayed the "send me" prayer that morning. It hit me like a thunder bolt, "It must be God!" I realized. "But why is He sending me to the mall? What could He want me to do for Him by getting a haircut?"

Yet when the thought immediately returned, "Go to the mall for a haircut," I got up, grabbed my coat, and headed for my car. I must confess that I was grumbling as I drove the short distance to the mall. "I wonder how much this haircut is going to cost? How will I explain to Cathy my sudden urge for extravagance? Why would God want me to go to the mall? Why couldn't God give me a more glamorous assignment?"

I walked into the hair salon and was given the only open chair. A young lady put a sheet around my neck and asked me how I wanted my hair cut. Then we engaged in small talk. As we did she asked me where I worked.

I told her that I was the campus pastor of the Christian university down the road.

"Oh my God!" she gasped. (I became worried at this point because she was holding scissors and I was unarmed.)

"I don't believe this!" she said as she started to cry. "This morning as I got ready for work I told God I would give Him one last chance. If He did not send me a Christian to talk to today, I was going to end it all tonight."

Now I understood why I was sent to the mall to get a haircut. As a result of our conversation she got her life back on track with God, and I gained a deep appreciation for the power of "send me" prayers.

"Send me" prayer is asking God to place you in a position of usefulness to Him and His Kingdom. It is seeking divine appointments to be a difference-maker in the lives of people. It is telling God you are willing to go where He wants you to go. It is letting Him deploy you as He sees fit. It is asking God to expand your ministry to others.

The most famous "send me" prayer was offered by the prophet Isaiah. It is recorded in the sixth chapter of the Book bearing his name.

In the year that King Uzziah died, I saw the Lord seated on a throne, high and exalted, and the train of His robe filled the temple. Above Him were seraphs, each with six wings: With two wings they covered their faces, with two they covered their feet, and with two they were flying. And they were calling to one another: "Holy, holy, holy is the Lord Almighty; the whole earth is full of His glory." At the sound of their voices the doorposts and thresholds shook and the temple was filled with smoke. "Woe to me!" I cried. "I am ruined! For I am a man of unclean lips, and I live among a people of unclean lips, and my eyes have seen the King, the Lord Almighty." Then one of the seraphs flew to me with a live coal in his hand, which he had taken with tongs from the altar. With it he touched my mouth and said, "See, this has touched your lips; your guilt is taken away and your sin atoned for." Then I heard the voice of the Lord saying, "Whom shall I send? And who will go for Us?" And I said, "Here am I. Send me!" (Isaiah 6:1-8)

Isaiah had an encounter with the Lord that gave him a passion to go tell others what God had done for him. So he made himself available. He asked for a commissioning. He prayed, "Here am I. Send me!"

I began writing this chapter on a Saturday morning at the end of the high school wrestling season. I wrote for a while that morning, and later, as I left to go watch my son wrestle, I prayed the "send me" prayer.

This tournament was the one that wrestlers needed to win in order to qualify for a place at the prestigious state tournament. My son was only a sophomore, but he had four seniors on his team who had a good chance at qualifying. All four had worked very hard to reach their goal.

The first guy lost his match and was crushed. I happened to sit down next to him about an hour later. He looked at me and said, "Mr. Earley, I don't know why this happened to me. I worked so hard. I said my prayers. I stayed out of trouble. I don't understand."

At that moment I remembered praying the "send me" prayer that morning. I looked at him and said, "Let me tell you a story." I told him how I had just missed qualifying for the state tournament at the end of my senior season. I told him how hurt I had felt after so much work. Then I explained how God used that event to steer me to a different college, and as a result I was called into the ministry and met the girl who would become my wife. I told him that it had hurt so badly that day but I appreciate it today. I reminded him that we need to live right because it is right, not in order to win wrestling matches.

He smiled and said, "Thank you. That makes sense. I am glad God sent you to talk to me today."

About two hours later the next senior lost a heartbreaking match in the last few seconds. He had missed qualifying for the state tournament by only 20 seconds! He was so hurt that he cried and yelled in anguish. Somehow things worked out so I was the only one around to talk to him. I said, "Let me tell you a story. When I was a senior I missed qualifying for the state tournament by one match." Then I told him how God had used that painful event to direct me to a different college and into the ministry. I reminded him that God loved him and we loved him whether he won or lost. This may have felt like death, but it was not life and death. He would live through it and become a better man for it.

After I had finished, he smiled and hugged me. He said, "I can't believe it! You understand how I feel right now."

About five minutes later the third senior came storming into the room with tears in his eyes. He had just lost the match he needed to win to qualify for the state tournament. Again I was the only adult there to talk to him. I sat down next to him and said, "Let me tell you a story…." Soon the guys and I were laughing and crying at the same time.

Then the fourth senior stormed in crying. He also had just lost the match he needed to win to qualify for the state tournament. I waited till he calmed down and sat next to him and said, "Let me tell you a story…."

The wonderful thing about that day was that, in the space of a few hours, I had been able to minister to four high school seniors at a highly vulnerable moment in their lives. Because of having gone through the same painful event they were experiencing and as a result of my relationship with them through my son, I had been divinely prepared to meet a need. God had sent me into their lives. The "send me" prayer had been answered.

In speaking about the adventure of requesting that God would use us, Bruce Wilkinson writes, "People will show up at your doorstep or at the table next to you. They will start saying things that surprise even them. They'll ask for something— they are not sure what—and wait for your reply."[1]

When God answers the "send me" prayer it is amazing to see how uniquely qualified God has made the person He sends to meet the assignment. God has shaped you to serve through your experiences, education, gifts, personality, and relationships. God has lives and situations that you are divinely prepared to touch.

I wonder what God has in store for you today. I am curious as to what adventure He may want to send you on, if you are willing to go. Ask God to send you today and be ready for an adventure into making a difference in people's lives.

ENDNOTES

1.Bruce Wilkinson, *The Prayer of Jabez* (Sisters, OR: Multnomah Publishers, 2000), p. 36.

Chapter 15

SHAMELESS, STUBBORN, PERSISTENT PRAYER

She had no choice. She was desperate and she was determined. Her adversary would not give her the money she was owed or refrain from harassing her. The godless, loveless judge was her only hope, so she went to him for justice. He refused, but she did not give up. Day after day, time after time she came to him for justice. It was his position. He had the obligation. He must work on her behalf. She was shameless and stubborn. She was persistent and persevering. And eventually she prevailed. Finally she wore him down. Finally she broke through. He could not take it anymore and said to himself, "Even though I don't fear God or care about men, yet because this widow keeps bothering me, I will see that she gets justice, so that she won't eventually wear me out with her coming!" (Luke 18:4-5) Her shameless stubborn persistence had won out.

Jesus told this story to teach us that we "should always pray and not give up" (Luke 18:1). He said that God will bring justice for His chosen ones who cry out to Him day and night. He will see that justice is given right away (see Luke 18:7-8).

Jesus told another parable in Luke 11:5-8 to teach persistence. He tells of a man who was awakened by the arrival of unexpected company late at night. The man wanted to be a good host and, obviously, there were no all-night grocery stores open in A.D. 30. So he marched over to his next-door neighbor's house, banged on the door, and yelled, "Friend, I have unexpected company. I am out of food. Lend me three loaves of bread."

His friend was unimpressed. He yelled back, "I'm in bed. Leave me alone."

Then Jesus said that even though the neighbor will not get out of bed to help because he is his friend, he *will* get up if the guy keeps pounding. Jesus said, "Because of the man's boldness he will get up and give him as much as he needs"

(Luke 11:8). The word He used for "boldness" could be translated "shamelessness" or "stubbornness." Jesus is advocating shameless stubborn persistence in prayer. In the very next verse He said, "*Ask and it will be given to you; seek and you will find; knock and the door will be opened to you*" (Luke 11:9).

When I was a Greek student in seminary, I learned that the Greek language was more technical than English. God chose Greek to be the language of the New Testament not just because it was the global language of commerce, but also because it conveyed fine shades of meaning. This is especially true when dealing with verbs and their tenses. For example, the present tense of continual action describes a much different meaning than the aorist tense of punctilliar action. If the verbs used in Matthew 7:7 and Luke 11:9—"ask," "seek," and "knock"—were aorist tense of punctilliar action they would express the notion of asking once and getting your answer. But they aren't. They are present tense, expressing continuing action. Therefore this verse could be understood as saying, "*Keep on* asking; *keep on* seeking; *keep on* knocking," and the answer will be given.

The man got his bread not because he was the friend of the neighbor, but because he kept on banging on his neighbor's door. He was shamelessly stubborn in his persistence, and his persistence prevailed where his friendship did not. His persistence was more powerful than his relationship.

———※———

Shameless, stubborn, persistent prayer is the prayer of *until*. It is persevering in your requests *until* God answers. It is continuing to come to God *until* the "Just Judge" gives you justice. It is knocking at the door of your truest Friend *until* He gives you the bread you need. It is prayer that keeps on asking, *until* it receives; keeps on seeking, *until* it finds; and keeps on knocking, *until* the door is opened.

The great praying evangelist D.L. Moody said, "If we knock, God has promised to open the door and grant our request. It may be years before the answer comes; He may keep us knocking; but He has promised that the answer will come."[1]

Moody told of a woman with an unsaved husband. She felt that God gave her a green light to ask for his salvation, so she resolved that she would pray every day for 12 months for his conversion. Every day at noon she would go to her room and pour her heart out to God on his behalf. Twelve months passed and there was no sign of his yielding to Christ. She resolved to pray six months longer. Six months passed and there was no answer. She said, "I will keep asking as long as God gives me breath."

One evening her husband came home and he went straight to the bedroom. When he did not come down for dinner she crept cautiously to the bedroom. Opening the door, she found him on his knees crying out to God. He went on to become a strong Christian.[2]

In Luke 18:1, when Jesus said that we should "always pray and not give up," He was not saying that we should pray every second. He was saying that once we start praying about something we should not give up after asking for it once. We should *keep on* asking. We are supposed to be like the widow in His story and keep coming to God until we get our answer. We must be persistent, stubbornly persistent, in our prayers. If you know that what you need is something God would like to give and can give, then ask for it and keep asking *until* you get it or *until* God leads you otherwise.

―――――⦿―――――

One of the greatest people of prayer the world has ever known was George Muller. Muller testified that he received over 10,000 answers to prayer. What was his secret? He tried to discover the will of God on a matter and then kept on asking *until* God answered.

In his lifetime Muller never asked anyone for help and never hinted that help was needed. Solely in answer to believing prayer, nearly $7,500,000 was sent to him for the building and maintenance of orphanages housing 10,000 orphans, for his missionary enterprises, and for the circulation of the Scriptures. He may have never asked man for help, but with God he was shamelessly stubborn in persisting prayer.

In his journal Muller recorded this example of persistence in prayer:

"In November, 1844, I began to pray for the conversion of five individuals. I prayed every day without a single intermission, whether sick or in health, on the land or on the sea, and whatever the pressure of my engagements might be. Eighteen months elapsed before the first of the five was converted. I thanked God and prayed on for the others. Five years elapsed, and then the second was converted. I thanked God for the second, and prayed on for the other three. Day by day I continued to pray for them, and six years passed before the third was converted. I thanked God for the three and went on praying for the other two."[3]

Years later, those two remained unconverted. Muller wrote:

"The man to whom God in the riches of his grace has given tens of thousands of answers to prayer in the self-same hour or day in which they were offered has been praying day by day for nearly 36 years for the conversion of these individuals, and yet they remain unconverted. But I hope in God, I pray on, and look yet for the answer. They are not converted yet, but they will be. I have not a doubt that I shall meet them both in heaven; for my Heavenly Father would not lay upon my heart a burden of prayer for them for over threescore years, if He had not concerning them purposes of mercy."[4]

And now for the rest of the story: In 1897 Muller died. After he had entreated God on their behalf daily for 52 years, those two men, sons of a friend of Mr. Muller's youth, were still not converted.

But one was converted at Muller's funeral and the other shortly thereafter![5]

——=•()•=——

Here are some other great quotes about persistent prayer.

1. Andrew Murray calls persistent prayer "the school of answer delayed." He says, "O what a deep heavenly mystery this is of persevering prayer.

The God who has promised, who longs, whose fixed purpose it is to give the blessing, holds it back. It is to Him a matter of such deep importance that His friends on earth should know and fully trust their rich Friend in heaven, that He trains them, in the school of answer delayed, to find out how their perseverance really does prevail, and what the mighty power is they can wield in heaven, if they do but set themselves to it."[6]

2. Adoniram Judson spent his life in persistent prayer. He said, "I never prayed sincerely and earnestly for anything but it came at some time; no matter at how distant a day, somehow, in some shape, it came."[7]

3. In his book *No Easy Road*, Dick Eastman says, "Answers always come if we never cease to pray."[8]

4. "The great point is never give up until the answer comes," according to George Muller.[9]

Often we sense that God is leading us to pray for something and we pray. But if we do not see answers quickly we get discouraged and quit. There are times we need to "pray *until*"— *until* God gives us our request or *until* He releases us from the burden to pray for it.

Are there some requests that you believe God wants to answer? Have you asked Him for them? Will you keep on asking, keep on seeking, keep on knocking until the answer comes or God tells you to quit? Will you "pray until"?

ENDNOTES

1. D.L. Moody, *Prevailing Prayer* (Chicago, IL: Moody Press, 1987), p. 94.

2. Ibid p. 96.

3. Basil Miller, *George Muller* (Minneapolis, MN: Bethany 4. Fellowship, 1943), p. 146.

4. Ibid.

5. Ibid.

6. Andrew Murray, *With Christ in the School of Prayer* (Grand Rapids, MI: Zondervan, 1983), p. 39.

7. Dick Eastman, *No Easy Road* (Grand Rapids, MI: Baker Book House, 1971), p. 98.

8. Ibid p. 53.

9. Ibid p. 97.

Chapter 16

STANDING TOGETHER PRAYER

Never underestimate the power of combined prayer. Like many dynamic spiritual truths, this truth is illustrated in the Old Testament.

The Hebrews had escaped from Egypt. They were hiking through the wilderness on their way to the Promised Land when a strong enemy attacked. It was the Amalekites.

Moses told Joshua to gather the men and prepare to fight them the next morning. With an army of untrained ex-slaves, Joshua had to face the army of the Amalckites. The odds of victory would have been slim.

As Joshua and the men went into the battle, Moses, Aaron, and Hur went to the top of the hill. Then a very unusual thing occurred.

As long as Moses held up his hands, the Israelites were winning, but whenever he lowered his hands, the Amalekites were winning. When Moses' hands grew tired, they took a stone and put it under him and he sat on it. Aaron and Hur held his hands up—one on one side, one on the other—so that his hands remained steady till sunset. So Joshua overcame the Amalekite army with the sword (Exodus 17:11-13).

Raising the hands is a sign of dependence in prayer (see 1 Tim. 2:8). As long as Moses held his hands up in prayer, Joshua and the Israelites were winning the battle. When Moses got tired and lowered his hands, Joshua and Israel were losing. When Aaron and Hur realized what was happening, they literally held Moses hands up with their arms and they spiritually held his hands up in prayer. Because the hands were held high in prayer, the battle was won.

Wow! Say it with me: Wow! Say it backward: Wow! The standing together prayers of those three men led the Israelites to their first military victory.

———※◎※———

Standing together prayer is praying *with* others for the same request. It may involve being with them physically or it may not, but it must include being united in spirit for the same request. Standing together prayer often involves being an instrument of an encounter with God and others that leads to powerful results.

———※◎※———

After years of being hammered by spiritual warfare, I came to understand the value of standing together prayer. It began when I recruited seven men to pray for me daily and especially on one day a week. Immediately the attacks lessened and every area of my life improved. The next year I recruited 31 men to pray for me daily, one special day a week, and one extra special day a month. I noticed another jump in the decrease of spiritual attacks and the increase of God's blessing on my life. Now I have about 50 men I call my "mighty men." They are my Aarons and Hurs. I would not have been able to stay victorious in the battle without them.

———※◎※———

In the New Testament, Jesus gave a great endorsement of standing together prayer. It includes two prerequisites and two awesome promises.

Again, I tell you that if two of you on earth agree about anything you ask for, it will be done for you by My Father in heaven. For where two or three come together in My name, there am I with them (Matthew 18:19-20).

Go back and read those verses again. Did you notice the prerequisites? The first is that they agree about what they are asking for. The second is that they come together in His name.

Did you notice the promises? The first is that the standing together prayers will receive a favorable answer. The second is that He will manifest His presence with them.

———— ❊ ————

Standing together prayer has always been a powerful tool in the hands of the Church of Jesus Christ. It was standing together prayer that birthed the Church on the day of Pentecost (see Acts 1–2). After Jesus ascended into Heaven, the 120 disciples prayed together in the upper room. Luke summarized their prayer meeting with these words: "They all joined together constantly in prayer, along with the women and Mary the mother of Jesus, and with His brothers" (Acts 1:14).

It was standing together prayer that opened prison doors and set Peter free. King Herod had set out to persecute the leaders of the early Church. He arrested James, the brother of John, and had him killed. Since this proved to be popular with the crowd, Herod arrested Peter as well and kept him in prison overnight. Look at what happened next: "So Peter was kept in prison, but the church was earnestly praying to God for him" (Acts 12:5).

Elsewhere in the chapter we find that many had gathered at the house of Mary, the mother of John Mark. They were not gathered to grieve, they were gathered to stand together in prayer. God responded to their standing together prayers in a wonderful way. Read what happened:

The night before Herod was to bring him to trial, Peter was sleeping between two soldiers, bound with two chains, and sentries stood guard at the entrance. Suddenly an angel of the Lord appeared and a light shone in the cell. He struck Peter on the side and woke him up. "Quick, get up!" he said, and the chains fell off Peter's wrists. Then the angel said to him, "Put on your clothes and sandals." And Peter did so. "Wrap your cloak around you and follow me," the angel told him. Peter followed him out of the prison, but he had no idea that what the angel was doing was really happening; he thought he was seeing a vision. They passed the first and second guards and came to the iron gate leading to the city. It opened for them by itself, and they went through it. When they had walked the length of one street, suddenly the angel left him. Then Peter came to himself and said, "Now I know without a doubt that the Lord sent His angel and rescued me from Herod's clutches and from everything the Jewish people were anticipating." When this had dawned on him, he went to the house of Mary the mother of John, also called Mark, where many peo-ple had gathered and were praying. Peter knocked at the outer entrance, and a servant girl named Rhoda came to answer the door. When she recognized Peter's voice, she was so overjoyed she ran back without opening it and exclaimed, "Peter is at the door!" "You're out of your mind," they told her. When she kept insisting that it was so, they said, "It must be his angel." But Peter kept on knocking, and when they opened the door and saw him, they were astonished (Acts 12: 6-16).

Peter's life was spared as Christians stood together in prayer. Never underesti-mate the power of combined prayer.

Maybe God is calling you to be serious in prayer for someone else *with* some-one else. Maybe this will be a one-time event, or perhaps a weekly commitment. Either way, standing together prayer can make a big difference.

Who might the Lord have for you to become linked in prayer with? If you are married, your prayer partner might be your mate. If you are not married, do not seek a prayer partner of the opposite sex as this can create unnecessary temptation.

Let me encourage you to pause right now and pray for a prayer partner or part-ners. Never underestimate the power of standing together prayer.

Chapter 17

STANDING IN THE GAP PRAYER

Moses left the Hebrews to go up on Mount Sinai to meet with God. He later returned with the Ten Commandments. However, when the people saw he was gone they got impatient. Not too long before this time, God had sent ten miraculous plagues on Egypt in order to free the Israelites from slavery but they weren't satisfied.

All the other nations had idols and Israel wanted to be like the other nations, so they asked Aaron to make them an idol. Foolishly, he did. He made them a golden calf. Then they threw a wild party to celebrate their new "god."

This did not please the true God. He told Moses that He was fed up with their disobedience. He was going to destroy them and make Moses and his children into a great nation.

Instead of agreeing with God and allowing God to make him great, Moses did something that made a big difference. He stood in the gap in prayer on their behalf:

But Moses sought the favor of the Lord his God. "O Lord," he said, "why should Your anger burn against Your people, whom You brought out of Egypt with great power and a mighty hand? Why should the Egyptians say, 'It was with evil intent that He brought them out, to kill them in the mountains and to wipe them off the face of the earth'? Turn from Your fierce anger; relent and do not bring disaster on Your people. Remember Your servants Abraham, Isaac and Israel, to whom You swore by Your own self: 'I will make your descendants as numerous as the stars in the sky and I will give your descendants all this land I promised them, and it will be their inheritance forever'" (Exodus 32:11-13).

Guess what? God heard his plea and did not destroy them: "Then the Lord relented and did not bring on His people the disaster He had threatened" (Exod. 32:14).

The story of Moses successfully standing in the gap for Israel is summarized in Psalm 106:23: "So He said He would destroy them—had not Moses, His chosen one, stood in the breach before Him to keep His wrath from destroying them."

Underline that phrase, "had not Moses"—now *that* is making a difference! God would have destroyed them "had not Moses stood in the gap." Wow! Say it with me: Wow! Say it backward, Wow! One man's prayers saved an entire nation.

Now circle the phrase, "stood in the breach." That could be translated "stood in the gap." The reason Moses was so mighty in prayer is because he prayed a "standing in the gap" prayer. He stood in the gap between God and the people. He stood between the wicked people and the Holy Lord God. He stood before God on behalf of the people to ask for the Lord's mercy. And he made a nation-saving difference!

Standing in the gap prayer is making a difference by going in prayer to a place between holy God and sinful people. It is selflessly standing before God *for* others. It is asking God to restrain judgment from others and show mercy to them.

In Genesis 18 we find that account of how God told Abraham of His plan to destroy the horribly wicked cities of Sodom and Gomorrah. Yet, Abraham stood before the Lord in prayer asking Him to spare Sodom and Gomorrah if there were but ten righteous people to be found in the entire place. And God agreed! (See Genesis 18:16-33.)

That is amazing! One man, standing in the gap in prayer, could have saved a whole city. He got God to agree to spare a vile, wicked place if only ten righteous people could be found. Sadly, there were not ten righteous people to be found in Sodom. So the wicked cities were destroyed. Nevertheless, the validity and power of Abraham's standing in the gap prayer was on display.

Standing in the gap prayer is persuading God to restrain judgment and show mercy. It is calling down the mercy of God when judgment is due.

Later on in the history of Israel, God warned that because of their rebellion He would withdraw His protection and let Israel try to survive on her own. If they did not want anything to do with God, God did not want anything to do with them. Then God said a most amazing thing: "I looked for a man among them who would build up the wall and stand before Me in the gap on behalf of the land so I would not have to destroy it, but I found none" (Ezek. 22:30).

Standing in the gap prayer is asking God to pour out His mercy on those who deserve it. It has the power to make a difference for nations and individuals.

You may not feel that you have the calling or authority to stand in the gap for a nation, but you can stand in the gap for individuals.

It has been said, "Prayer is the soul of man stirred to plead with God for men."[1] Dick Eastman has written, "To intercede is to mediate. It is to stand between a lost being and an almighty God, praying that this person will come to know about God and his salvation."[2]

We must never underestimate the potential impact of our standing in the gap prayer for others. A.T. Pierson has stated, "Every step in the progress of missions is directly traceable to prayer. It has been the preparation for every triumph and the secret of all success."[3] Eastman adds, "Search for a person who claims to have found Christ apart from someone else's prayer, and your search may go on forever."[4]

Is there someone God is bringing to mind whose rebellion has made him or her a candidate for God's judgment? Will you heed the Spirit's call to stand in the gap for them right now?

ENDNOTES

1. E.M. Bounds as quoted by Dick Eastman in *The Hour That Changes the World* (Grand Rapids, MI: Baker Book House, 1978), p. 76.

2. Ibid p. 76.

3. Ibid p. 79.

4. Ibid p. 76.

Chapter 18

"SEND REVIVAL" PRAYER

Jeremiah Lamphier was a young man who had a heart for God. In 1857 the United States was on the verge of an awful war and the economy was crumbling. Instead of worrying or whining about the problems, he decided to pray about them. He printed handbills and passed them out in the area. The handbills stated that he was starting a noon prayer meeting in the banking district of Manhattan in New York City.

On the first day, September 23, at noon no one had showed up, so he began to pray alone. He asked God to send revival. By the time he had finished praying that day, six men had joined him. Two days later the Bank of Philadelphia failed. The next week 20 people turned out to pray.

On October 7th there were 40 people at the prayer meeting, so they decided to pray together daily at noon. On October 10 the stock market crashed. The financial panic triggered a renewed desperation for God and people flocked to the prayer meetings. Within six months nearly 10,000 people were gathering daily for prayer in New York City alone. The "send revival" prayers of one young man sparked a citywide revival!

According to revival historian Wesley Duewel, "The meetings abounded with love for Christ, love for fellow Christians, love for prayer, and love of witnessing. Those in attendance felt an awesome sense of God's presence. They prayed for specific people, expected answers, and obtained answers."[1]

Soon the media got a hold of the story and news of the revival quickly traveled westward by telegraph. Lay people organized interdenominational prayer meetings in cities across the East Coast. Unlike earlier awakenings, prayer, rather than preaching, was the main instrument of revival.

What began in the cities spread to towns, villages, rural areas, colleges, and schools. The "send revival" prayers of one young man sparked a national revival! Duewel reports,

"For six to eight weeks during the height of the revival, some fifty thousand people were converted weekly. The average for the two years [1857-1859] was ten thousand new converts joining the churches each week. The Washington National Intelligencer reported that in several New England towns not a single unconverted person could be found."[2]

This was the first revival beginning in America that had a worldwide impact. From the United States the revival spread to Ireland, Scotland, Wales, England, Europe, South Africa, India, Australia, and the Pacific islands. In geographical and proportionate numerical extent, the revival of 1857-1860 has not been equaled. The "send revival" prayers of one young man sparked a worldwide revival!

When Pastor Andrew Bonar heard of the work, he increased his prayer for a revival in Scotland. In his diary of July 3, 1859, he wrote, "Again this night in sorrow of heart over the terrible carelessness, indifference, deadness of this 'valley of dry bones.' O my God, come over to Scotland and help us!"[3]

Within two months Andrew Bonar found himself in the midst of revival in Scotland. On September 10th he wrote in his diary, "This has been a remarkable week: every day I have heard of some soul saved among us…."[4] All classes of people became interested in salvation. Backsliders returned, conversions increased, and Christians desired a deeper instruction in spiritual truths. Families established daily devotions, and entire communities underwent a noticeable change in morals.

Similar changes were noted as the revival spread to Wales, England, and beyond…lay people in prayer were the prime instruments used by God in awakening the people. The results of the revival of 1859 in the areas of evangelism, missions, and social action continued for decades. As James Buchanan of Scotland summarized, it was a time when "new spiritual life was imparted to the dead, and new spiritual health imparted to the living."[5]

Wow! The prayers of one young man made a big difference!

"Send revival" prayer is asking God to come and work in unusual, unprecedented fashion. It may involve seeking revival for a church, a city, a school, a denomination, or a nation. It begins by drawing a circle around yourself and asking God to revive or bring fresh life to your soul. It is based on this promise:

If My people, who are called by My name, will humble themselves and pray and seek My face and turn from their wicked ways, then will I hear from heaven and will forgive their sin and will heal their land (2 Chronicles 7:14).

"Send revival" prayer is predicated on our willingness to humble ourselves before the loftiness of Almighty God. It requires our willingness to allow ourselves to become broken before His holiness.

For this is what the high and lofty One says—He who lives forever, whose name is holy: "I live in a high and holy place, but also with him who is contrite and lowly in spirit, to revive the spirit of the lowly and to revive the heart of the contrite (Isaiah 57:15).

"Send revival" prayer is not complicated. It may be the result of very simple prayers. One such scriptural example is found in Psalm 85:6: "Will You not revive us again, that Your people may rejoice in You?"

I believe that just as God used a young man with a burning heart to spark a worldwide revival in 1857, He wants to do the same today. There are some young men and women—and some not-so-young men and women—reading this book who could be the human instruments of divine visitations. Is God calling you to be a difference-maker through "send revival" prayer? Will you hear His call and pray?

ENDNOTES

1. Wesley Duewel, *Revival Fire* (Grand Rapids, MI: Zondervan Publishing House, 1995), p. 129.
2. Ibid, p. 131.
3. Ibid.
4. Ibid.
5. Ibid.

Chapter 19

SPIRITUAL WARFARE PRAYER

Pain. Sharp, stinging pain. I tossed and turned, quickly realizing that no matter how I laid, I had no hope of getting comfortable. I got out of bed and looked down at my arm. Every painful area was marked with an angry red welt. My legs and back were worse, burning red welts everywhere.

"Twenty-one!" the doctor exclaimed shaking his head. "Twenty-one boils."

"I have had only one boil in my life," I said. "How could I get twenty-one all at the same time?"

He proceeded to quiz me on everywhere I had been recently, everything I had done, and everything I had eaten. "Uh, uh," he sighed, shaking his head. (I don't like it when doctors shake their heads).

"Never seen anything like it…so many boils coming so fast," he muttered. "Never read anything like it…except in the Book of Job." The light of insight flashed in his eyes. "This is a long shot but it is worth asking. What are you preaching on Sunday?" (My doctor is a believer.)

"Spiritual warfare," I said. "I am preaching on the devil and demons."

"Bingo!" he said. "This can only be spiritual warfare."

The coming of the boils and the visit to the doctor had happened on a Tuesday. I went home from the doctor's and told Cathy what he had said. She called some of our prayer warriors and asked them to pray for a miracle.

Friday morning I was back at the doctor's. "Gone," he muttered shaking his head. "All gone. Never seen anything like it. Boils don't come and go that quickly. Your people must have done some spiritual warfare on your behalf."

Within two days all of the boils were all gone. Wow! Say it with me: Wow! Say it backward: Wow! Spiritual warfare prayer made the difference.

Spiritual warfare prayer calls God into action against satan and his demons. It protects God's people from the enemy. It is prayer that God uses to invade enemy territory and establish His Kingdom.[1] It can hinder, detain, or derail the enemy's efforts on planet earth. Spiritual warfare stirs or stops battles between angels and demons in the unseen world of the heavenlies (see Dan. 10:1-14).

Finally, be strong in the Lord and in His mighty power. Put on the full armor of God so that you can take your stand against the devil's schemes. For our struggle is not against flesh and blood, but against the rulers, against the authorities, against the powers of this dark world and against the spiritual forces of evil in the heavenly realms (Ephesians 6:10-12).

How do we stand against the devil's schemes? Defensively we make sure we have our armor on. But how do we wage war offensively? The answer comes later in the passage: "And pray in the Spirit on all occasions with all kinds of prayers and requests" (Eph. 6:18).

One of the primary weapons of warfare against the enemy is prayer. Note that it is praying with "all kinds of prayers." All 31 flavors of prayer annoy, irritate, frustrate, and hinder the enemy. But the rest of the passage gives us even more insight into spiritual warfare prayer: "...With this in mind, be alert and always keep on praying for all the saints" (Eph. 6:18).

Paul talks about being "alert." The idea here is that we develop both a spiritual maturity, which gives us the ability to not be ignorant of the devil's schemes (see 2 Cor. 2:11), and a spiritual sensitivity to be aware of what, where, and how he is working. Once we see what is happening we are to "always keep on praying." In my case, my doctor was "alert" to the fact that sometimes satan attacks our physical health, and the people in my church "kept on praying."

Paul continues by saying that we need to not just do spiritual warfare prayer for ourselves, but "for all the saints." I think warfare prayer is often most effective when we selflessly pray for others, since the devil hates unselfish sacrifice.

Paul gives further insight into warfare prayer when he writes:

Pray also for me, that whenever I open my mouth, words may be given me so that I will fearlessly make known the mystery of the gospel, for which I am an ambassador in chains. Pray that I may declare it fearlessly, as I should (Ephesians 6:19-20).

If the enemy can defeat a shepherd he can get at the flock more easily. Therefore pastors and other Christian leaders have a bull's-eye on their backs and they especially need our prayers.

———◦(◦)◦———

When we first started our church I was ignorant of the enemy's schemes, and the enemy took advantage of that. Every Saturday was miserable at my house, especially if we had a big crowd expected on Sunday morning. The kids would be healthy all week but wake up vomiting on Saturday night. Or they would be good all week and be rotten on Saturday night. Or my wife and I would get along great all week and get in an argument over some stupid little thing on Saturday night. Plus at about 12:30 a.m. every Saturday night, right after we had fallen asleep, the phone would ring. It would either be a wrong number or a drunk.

After a few years of this I began to see a pattern. (I am a little slow.) So I swallowed my pride and one Sunday night I explained to my people what was going on and asked them to pray for me every Saturday night. The next Saturday night was heaven in my home. The kids were good and healthy. Cathy and I got along great. The phone did not ring. I slept like a baby. And that Sunday I preached better than ever. (Now, I tell my church that if they want me to preach better messages they need to pray better prayers.)

Since then I have developed a team of 50 men who make a one-year commitment to pray for me daily. I also have a team of men who pray for me every Sunday when I am preaching. Because they are guys, I use a football image to help them understand their importance. I call them the offensive line and tell them their job is to block the enemy. I can't throw touchdowns if they don't block. As the quarterback I cannot effectively do my job (throw the touchdown pass), if they don't do theirs (block the enemy through their prayers). I may get more credit when things go well and more blame when things go poorly, but when someone gets saved or set free, we all will get championship rings in Heaven.

I also tell them prayer is reciprocal. When they pray for God to bless my marriage, God not only blesses my marriage, He blesses their marriage. When they ask God to bless my kids, God not only blesses mine, He blesses theirs. When they lift up my health or finances or ministry, God blesses theirs.

Do you need to practice spiritual warfare prayer? Do you need to pray against the enemy's schemes in your life or in the lives of your family members? Do you need to begin lifting up your pastor in prayer? Maybe you should begin praying daily for your pastor. Maybe you can pray a little extra this Saturday night for the rest and protection of those who minister in your church on Sunday.

ENDNOTES

1. I have gained my best understanding of spiritual warfare prayer from the classic little book by S.D. Gordon, *Quiet Talks on Prayer* reprinted in 1980 (Grand Rapids, MI: Baker Book House) from the 1904 edition issued by Fleming H. Revell Company. Some of his best quotes include: "Now prayer is this: a man on the earth with his life in full touch with the Victor and sheer out of touch with the pretender-prince, insistently claiming that Satan shall yield before Jesus' victory, step by step, life after life" (p. 47), and "The scriptural standpoint always is this: that things quite outside of oneself, that in the natural order of prevailing circumstances would not occur, are made to occur through prayer" (p. 41).

Part 4
Depth Prayers

Chapter 20

STILLNESS PRAYER

I was always an active kid. I spent much of my early elementary years in the corner or visiting with the principal simply because I could not keep still. I remember once when my mom came home from open house. The first thing she said was, "Dave, why didn't you tell me where your desk was?"

I said, "I did, next to the teacher's."

She shook her head and sighed, "Yes, but when you said 'next to the teacher's,' I thought you meant the front row. I did not think you meant right up *next* to the teacher's."

In first or second grade the girl who sat in front of me was about six feet tall. Her name was Patricia—not Patty, oh no, *Patricia*. She was one of those always perfect, always clean, always quiet, straight-A, teacher's pet types. (You know the type. Maybe some of you were that type.) I wasn't. I got bored too easily. I was always saying, "Hey Patricia, look at that. Hey Patricia, watch this."

And probably a dozen times every day she would turn around and say, "Keep still, Dave Earley. You won't learn anything. Keep still." I can still hear her voice telling me, "Keep still."

The best day of first grade was the one time Patricia Gallagher ever got in trouble…because she was turned around talking…she was telling *someone* to keep still.

Do you know what? There are times I hear God in His deep baritone voice say, "Dave, keep still. You won't learn anything. Quiet your soul, Son. Slow down. Get off the fast lane. Jump off the treadmill. Stop doing. Start being. Be still."

I wonder, does God ever say to you, "Be still. I can't do anything with you because your world is too busy, too cluttered, too crowded, and too loud. You are busy about many things and you are neglecting that one thing that is most needful.

Your world is too loud to hear My voice. It is too cluttered to see My hand. It is too crowded to feel My touch"?

It is at these times we need to learn stillness/silence prayer.

One of the more challenging truths I have read in the last few years comes from the pen of John Ortberg on a subject he calls "slowing." He writes, "Jesus urged his disciples to take time out. Following Jesus cannot be done at a sprint. If we want to follow someone, we can't go faster than the one who is leading."[1]

Stillness prayer is ceasing physical activity so that we may experience spiritual growth. It is being still, so that we might know God. Stillness prayer is not so much the absence of noise as it is the presence of the divine whisper. It is being silent before God so we might listen to God. Silence prayer is creating space in our crowded souls in order that God may fill them with Himself.

A few years ago when I was preparing a message on Psalm 46, one particular phrase jumped off the page and grabbed my heart: "Be still, and know that I am God" (Ps. 46:10).

The word translated "know" can be understood as "experience." So in other words, this verse says, "Be still and experience God." As I read this verse, I realized that at the very point where my heart is not still, I am not experiencing God. At the very point where my heart is not still, I am not hearing God. God speaks through a still small voice. At the very point where I am not still, I am unable to see God or feel God. I realized that until I learned the prayer of stillness, I would not experience God as much, or as much of God, as I desired.

Stillness prayer is not so much the absence of noise as it is the presence of the divine whisper. It is being silent before God so that we might listen to God.

＝⊃⦅◉⦆⊂＝

There are times when I hear God say in my heart, "Be quiet. Stop talking. Stop thinking. Just listen. You are not ready to hear My voice until you are quiet enough to hear My heartbeat. Can you hear it? It is beating out love and strength and encouragement to you."

Until you are still enough to hear God's heartbeat, you will struggle to recognize God's voice. Let me repeat that. Until you are still enough to hear God's heartbeat, you will struggle to recognize God's voice.

Have you ever heard the heartbeat of God? When was the last time you heard God's heartbeat?

Stillness prayer is creating space in our crowded souls so that God may fill them with Himself.[2] Our hearts get so crowded—crowded with worries, fears, frustrations; crowded with wants and desires and wishes; crowded with good things, crowded with bad things. But whatever it is, it can easily crowd out God and drown out His voice.

This past summer I spent 48 hours in silence and stillness with God. I was in a hotel room in a distant city. At first it was uncomfortable. It was hard for me to get truly still. It was hard for me to just be quiet before God.

Writing in my journal, I slowly and silently worked through several types of prayer: adoration, confession, thanksgiving, and surrender. As I reached a certain level of stillness, the Holy Spirit began to unload my crowded heart. It felt awkward, yet very good, to sense Him carrying burdens out of my soul and off of my shoulders. I struggled with a sense of uneasiness because I was making nothing happen, yet something was definitely happening.

As my heart became less crowded, God became more real. His presence tenderly, quietly, peacefully began to flow into the newly vacated areas of my soul. I began to discern God's heart beating slowly, deeply, firmly, pounding out love and hope with each beat. His still small voice gave me an encouragement and a plan for the next chapter in my life. As I experienced a great calming in my soul, I realized just how tense, stressed, anxious, busy, cluttered, and empty I had let myself become in the previous months.

The best part of my 48 hours of silence and stillness was not the 48 hours themselves, although they were wonderful. The best part was the space that had been created during those 48 hours. I now had more room for God. For months afterward, I felt, heard, and tasted God more often, more deeply, and more clearly than before.

Since those blessed 48 hours I have tried to carry stillness prayer in my busy life. I had previously taken time each week to fast from food and have an appointment with God. Now I added stillness and silence to the plan. So one or two mornings a month, I get alone and quiet. I say as few words as possible. I try to use the time to practice stillness prayer. I cease physical activity that I may experience spiritual growth. I get outwardly and inwardly still, that I might experience God. I reduce noise in order to hear the divine whisper. I allow God to create space in my crowded soul so that God may fill me with Himself.

I also try to return to this mental/spiritual state of mind through the day and the week, but I will discuss that further under "sanctuary of the soul prayer."

Do you need to be still so that you might better experience God? Do you need to experience silence so you can hear God's voice? Do you need to create space so God can fill it?

Stop. Be still. Don't speak. Close your eyes. Slowly inhale God's presence and exhale the clutter in your soul. Smile and enjoy this precious little "God moment." If you have time, carry it deeper into your heart. Be still and experience God.

ENDNOTES

1. John Ortberg, *The Life You've Always Wanted* (Grand Rapids, MI: Zondervan Publishing House, 1997), p. 84.
2. Richard Foster as quoted in Richard Foster and Emilie Griffin, *Spiritual Classics: Selected Reading for Individuals and Groups on the Twelve Disciplines,* (New York, NY: HarperCollins Publishers, 2000), p. 158-159. Richard Foster has noted that the disciplines of silence, solitude, and stillness have the power to create "the emotional and spiritual space, which allows Christ to construct an inner sanctuary of the heart." What this means is that these disciplines are to be used "to create a space in our lives where God can reach us. Once that space has been created we wait quietly, expectantly. From this point on, the work belongs to God. And I have found Him most eager to usher us into the Holy of Holies and share with us the glories of His Kingdom."

Chapter 21

SANCTUARY OF THE SOUL PRAYER

As a student Thomas Kelly said to a professor, "I am going to make my life a miracle." From then on he set impossibly high standards for his life. He worked tirelessly to become a successful pastor, scholar, and professor. Yet, by the age of 43, his feverish efforts had driven him to exhaustion.

It was at this low point that he had an experience *with* God that ended the strain in his striving. He changed his focus to developing his relationship with God instead of acquiring more knowledge *about* God. His discovery blossomed into what could be called "sanctuary of the soul prayer."

Let me confess that I am a beginner in understanding and practicing the sanctuary of the soul prayer. Yet, it is one of the 31 flavors I need most dearly. Too often I feel the pull of many obligations and the frustration of trying to fulfill them all. Too easily I become unhappy, uneasy, strained, oppressed, and fearful. As a Christian I know that inner hint that there is a way of life vastly richer and deeper than all of this hurried existence, a life of unhurried serenity and peace and power. Yet, I wrestle to live it.

In his classic work, *A Testament of Devotion*, Kelly wrote,

"Deep within us all there is an amazing inner sanctuary of the soul, a holy place, a Divine Center, a speaking voice to which we may continuously return. Eternity is at our hearts, pressing upon our time-torn lives, warming us with intimations of astounding destiny, calling us home unto Itself…. It is the Shekinah of the soul, the Presence in the midst."[1]

[When we make our hearts a sanctuary] "of adoration and joy, thanksgiving and worship, self-surrender and listening. The secret places of the heart cease to be our busy workshop. They become a holy sanctuary of adoration and self-oblation, where we are kept in perfect peace."[2]

"There is a way of ordering our mental life on more than one level at once. On one level we may be meeting all the demands of external affairs. But deep within, behind the scenes, at a profounder level, we may also be in prayer and adoration, song and worship and gentle receptiveness to divine breathings."[3]

From what I understand, sanctuary of the soul prayer is an internal practice and habit of the mind of an increasing orientation of the depths of our being toward God. It is conducting our inward life so that we are perpetually bowed in worship, surrendering and listening, while we are very busy in the world of daily affairs. It is an inner secret turning to God made steady after weeks, months, and years of practice, lapses, failures, and returns. It is making a private chapel of our hearts where we can retire from time to time to commune with Him, peacefully, humbly, and lovingly. It is inwardly bringing our quiet times with God along with us out into the noisy world. It is learning how to carry God with us into the world in order to make a difference in the world.

<hr />

I am a highly competitive person. I have three active boys who have played many sports. I love sports. I often coach their teams. Added together, this is a potentially highly combustible combination. When a referee makes a bad call, or a parent or coach from the other team acts like a jerk, my buttons get pushed. Too often I find myself saying something I later regret. This is especially bad because not only am I a Christian, I happen to pastor the largest church in town. People know who I am. So, you can see, I need sanctuary of the soul prayer.

Happily, I can report that I am making progress. I am learning to take my still times with God into my loud life. I am seeing progress in practicing the serenity of silence and solitude during the chaos of a sporting event. Instead of wanting to break a "blind" ref's neck, I am learning to quietly pray for his soul. Instead of talking back to a player's mouthy mother, I am asking God to bless her marriage. Instead of scheming against the other coach, I am trying to handle myself in a way that will allow me to invite him and his family to church on Sunday.

I also have an oversensitive awareness of injustice, and I happen to live in a city with traffic issues and many construction areas. This is also a highly combustible combination. When I am driving home and I see someone cut in ahead of someone who has been waiting or deliberately cut off another person, it really bothers me. I want to yell at the offender or shoot their tires with a dart gun. When I have to wait for two minutes at a light because the road has too much traffic because someone did a poor job planning for the expansion of the city, I feel violated. I want to make the city planners spend one entire weekend a month just sitting in their cars at red lights. When I see someone throw trash out of their car window, I want to honk my horn and ram their vehicle and make them go back and pick it up. Obviously, I need sanctuary of the soul prayer.

I am learning to retire into the sanctuary of my soul for prayer as I sit at a ridiculously long red light. I am learning to pray for the city leaders and their families as I wait in traffic. I am learning to pray for the mates and children of offensive drivers. And it makes a difference. Instead of getting home bent out of shape, I get home with a sense of spiritual refreshment and renewal. Thank God for sanctuary of the soul prayer.

Kelly offers several insights into acquiring this sanctuary of the soul. I find it helpful that he describes it as a secret habit, a practice, and a perpetual return:

> "What is urged are secret habits of unceasing orientation of the depths of our being…so we are perpetually bowed in worship while we are very busy in the world of daily affairs. What is urged are inward practices of the mind at the deepest levels, letting it swing like a needle to the polestar of the soul."[4]

How? By quiet, persistent practice in turning all of our being, day and night, in prayer and inward worship and surrender, toward Him who calls in the depths of our

souls. Mental habits of inward orientation must be established. An inner, secret turning to God can be made fairly steady, after weeks and months and years of practice.[5]

Begin now as you read these words, as you sit in your chair, to offer your whole
selves, utterly and in joyful abandon, in quiet, glad surrender to Him who is within. In secret utterances of praise, turn in humble wonder to the Light…. Walk and
talk and work and laugh with your friends, but behind the scenes, keep up the life
of simple prayer and inward worship. Let inward prayer be your last act before you
fall asleep and the first act when you awake.[6]

The goal would be to reach the place where we can honestly say,

"The currents of his love have been flowing, but whereas we had been
drifting in him, now we swim…. We cease trying to make ourselves the
dictators and God the listener, and become joyful listeners to Him, the
Master who does all things well."[7]

We know we are experiencing sanctuary of the soul prayer when we enter a "stage
where the soul in its deeper levels is continuously at Home in Him." In order for this
to occur, Kelly advises us that "the conscious cooperation of the surface level is needed at first, before prayer sinks into the second level as divine orientation."[8]

We all have a struggle to carry our quiet times with God along with us out into
the noisy world. We wrestle with how to carry God with us into the world in order
to make a difference in the world. One way to get there is sanctuary of the soul
prayer.

Take the next few moments and become aware of the sanctuary in your soul.
Quietly clear some space in your soul and ask God to fill it. As you go through your
day, frequently return to the sanctuary and pause to surrender, worship, praise, and
pray. As you do, you will expand the eternity in your heart and enjoy the God who
reigns there.

ENDNOTES

1. Thomas R. Kelly, *A Testament of Devotion* (San Francisco, CA:
HarperSanFrancisco, 1941), p. 3.

2. Ibid, p. 4.

3. Ibid, p. 9.

4. Ibid, p. 5.

5. Ibid, pp. 11-12.

6. Ibid, p. 13.

7. Ibid, p. 7.

8. Ibid, p. 16.

Chapter 22

STUDENT PRAYER

That hour quickly became the highlight of my day. During my freshman year in college I made a commitment to spend an hour each day, starting at noon, with God in the Word and prayer. During my "hour of power" it seemed as though God would speak to me daily through His Word. No matter what I was going through, He would address it through the Scriptures I happened to be studying that day.

Daily I unearthed a fresh treasure from the Word of God. Every day, I ate meat, milk, and bread for my hungry soul as I consumed true "soul food." I discovered a lamp unto my feet and a light unto my path (see Ps. 119:105). I came to a better understanding of God, life, and myself. My faith grew, and my character was changed little by little, more and more, into the image of Jesus.

As I invested this time praying and studying the Bible, I fell hopelessly and permanently in love with the Bible and with the God of the Bible. I used to literally run from class to get back to my dorm at exactly noon to have my time with God each day. It was such an awesome time that I would skip lunch two or three days a week just to make sure I did not miss my full hour with God in His Word and prayer.

My plan was simple. I would spend half an hour studying a psalm each day and half an hour in systematic prayer. I had a spiral notebook where I recorded my insights from Psalms and a three-ring binder where I kept my prayer journal. Those two items, plus my Bible and a small commentary on the Psalms, became my four most prized possessions.

As I recall those early times with God, I can still see myself rushing into the dorm room and hanging up my coat. I remember feeling like a country doctor laying out his tools before a simple operation as I sat down at the desk and got out my tools: the Bible, my royal-blue spiral notebook for Bible study notes, my burgundy prayer notebook, and my commentary of the Psalms.[1] As I think back to those first days in the Word, I can still feel the anxious anticipation I felt then as I would close my eyes and take a deep breath and begin to meet with God.

I now realize that the next thing I did was one of the keys to my wonderful times spent with God in His Word. It is what I call the "student prayer." It is a little Scripture prayer that can make a big difference. "Open my eyes that I may see wonderful things in Your law" (Ps. 119:18).

Each day I would ask God to open my spiritual eyes so I could see what He had for me in His Word that day. Each day God would answer my prayer.

Student prayer is asking God to enlighten the eyes of our hearts as we open His Word. It is asking God to open our eyes that we might see the wondrous truths He has revealed for us in His Word and understand how they apply to our lives.

Student prayer is enhanced by good, commonsense plans and principles for Bible reading and Bible study. I want to give you three sets of guidelines that have made the student prayer work in my time in God's Word.

First, there are some general guidelines that enhance any daily time spent with God's Word:

1. *Have a set time.* My initial time was noon. Through the years I have had my time after work or before bed, but mostly I have it first thing in the morning.

2. *Block out an amount of time.* This may be from 10 minutes to an hour. Reading three chapters a day takes approximately 15-30 minutes, depending on the length of the chapters. By reading three chapters a day you can read through the Bible in a little over a year.

3. *Have a place.* My initial place was the desk of my dorm room. My current place is my green chair in the living room.

4. *Always start with the student prayer.*

There are also several guidelines that aid your Bible-reading time. These include:

1. *Follow a plan.* Some people like to read all the way through the Bible. Some like to jump around. I just finished reading two psalms a day. Prior to that, I read the Gospel of Mark. Before that, I read Kings and Chronicles. Before that I read Galatians every day, over and over for several weeks. Then it was the greatest events in the life of Jesus. Over the years, I have compiled several Bible-reading plans that can be checked off each day.[2]

2. *Read till God speaks. Then stop.*

3. *Do not continue to read if God is speaking to you.* Stay there until God is done. This may take just a few moments or several minutes. There is no need to take in more until you have fully taken in what you have already been given.

4. *Mark it in your Bible or write it in your notebook.* What you note may be a sin you need to confess, a promise you need to claim, an example you need to follow, or a command you should keep. Thank God for "opening your eyes." After you have "got it" and said "Thanks," read on.

5. *Do not worry about getting it all read.* I generally read two to three chapters a day. But if one is loaded with stuff I need, I simply take all of my daily allotted time to fully enjoy that one chapter.

6. *As you read, do not be afraid to underline, circle, or mark key words, names, or verses in your Bible.*

7. *Read in different translations on occasion.*

8. *Vary your "diet" by periodically switching from reading the Old Testament to the New and vice versa.* It is all the Word of God.

Some of the basics that I find most helpful for Bible study include:

1. Have a plan. My first plan was to study a psalm a day.

2. Have your tools. My tools were my Bible, my notebook, a commentary on the Psalms, and a pen.

3. Take three steps:

Step One: Observation. Read the passage and ask yourself, "What does this passage say? What is the author saying? Who wrote this passage? Who were they writing to? Why were they writing? The first passage I studied was in the Psalms.

Step Two: Interpretation. Take each passage in chunks of sentences or paragraphs. As you look at it, answer the question: "What did the author intend for this to mean?" I often would paraphrase it into my own words.

Step Three: Application. Be able to finish this sentence: "Based on what this says, I should…." It may be in terms of a sin you need to confess, a promise you need to claim, an example you need to follow, or a command you need to keep.

ENDNOTES

1. My first commentary on the Psalms was Derek Kidner's, *The Tyndale Old Testament Commentary, Psalms 1-72* (London: InterVarsity Press, 1973).

2. I have included nearly a dozen Bible-reading plans, along with the basics of my prayer notebook, in *Prime Time: A Daily Guide for Spending Time with God,* which is currently available through our church bookstore. Call us at New Life Church: (614) 475-8500.

Chapter 23

SCRIPTURE PRAYER

Weak and cranky—that's how I feel when I get hungry. I have a high metabolism and try to exercise about an hour a day. I also don't take time for breakfast. By about 10 a.m. I can get really hungry, very weak, and highly cranky, so I eat a piece of fruit or some nuts. Instantly I feel better, stronger, and happier.

As Christians, sometimes we wonder why we are weak and cranky spiritually. Often the answer is that we need to eat spiritually.

At one point in His life Jesus was fasting for 40 days and nights. The Bible says that He was hungry (see Matt. 4:2). Satan came and tempted Him saying, "If you are really God then turn these rocks into bread." Then Jesus said an amazing thing.

Jesus answered, "It is written: 'Man does not live on bread alone, but on every word that comes from the mouth of God' " (Matthew 4:4).

According to Jesus, the spiritual food for the believer is the Word of God. Jesus was not alone in His view that the Bible is the "soul food" of the believer. Job also saw the Bible as spiritual food when he said, "I have treasured the words of His mouth more than my daily bread" (Job 23:12).

In speaking of the words of God, David wrote, "They are more precious than gold, than much pure gold; they are sweeter than honey, than honey from the comb" (Ps. 19:10).

Jeremiah wrote, "When Your words came, I ate them; they were my joy and my heart's delight, for I bear Your name, O Lord God Almighty" (Jer. 15:16).

Ezekiel wrote, "Then He said to me, 'Son of man, eat this scroll I am giving you and fill your stomach with it.' So I ate it, and it tasted as sweet as honey in my mouth" (Ezek. 3:3).

Peter said, "As newborn babes, desire the pure milk of the word, that you may grow thereby" (1 Pet. 2:2 NKJV).

In order to really be a physically healthy person one must eat regularly and properly. In order to be a spiritually healthy person, one must eat of the Word of God regularly. The problem with most of us is that we have overfed bellies and underfed souls. One of the best ways to feed on the soul food of the Word of God is to pray the Scriptures. One of the best ways to go to a new level in your Christian life, your prayer life, and your Bible study life is to learn to pray the Bible.

Scripture prayer is making the words of Scripture the content of your prayers. It is speaking God's Word back to Him. It is reciting or reading the Scripture slowly, deeply, and repeatedly until you have sensed the very heart of what you have read. It is feeding on the Word until it becomes your necessary food, your daily bread, your meat, and your milk. Scripture prayer is going a step beyond student prayer. It is not just praying about your study of the Scriptures. It is making the Scriptures the very content of your prayers.

Every three months God seems to give me a passage of Scripture that especially applies to my situation. I read it, study it, and memorize it. But it does not become mine until I pray it. Every day I spend some time praying the heart of that passage back to God and applying it to my needs. Every day I chew it a little more and get more nutrients out of it. As I add a new passage every season—winter, spring, summer, and fall—I continue praying the previous ones until I feel released from the need to do so.

For example, at this time I seem to have an unprecedented number of large, unresolved situations. I could easily get anxious about all these things. But I have been praying the Scripture: "And we know that in all things God works for the good of those who love Him, who have been called according to His purpose" (Rom. 8:28).

Every day, I review these unresolved issues with the Lord, telling Him that I believe He is working them for good. Four words from that verse have become the core of my prayers: "all things...for good." Throughout the day, I ask God to indeed work all things for good. Since I began doing this a few months ago, I have seen God at work in every issue and have already seen positive resolution to some of them.

The season previous to this one, I was burdened about seeing several doors open for greater ministry opportunities. I prayed Matthew 7:7, "Ask and it will be given to you; seek and you will find; knock and the door will be opened to you." Those last five words, "the door will be opened," became the meat of my prayers as I asked God to open several doors in my life. Currently I am seeing how He is answering that prayer.

Prior to that, my passage was:

"Have faith in God," Jesus answered. "I tell you the truth, if anyone says to this mountain, 'Go, throw yourself into the sea,' and does not doubt in his heart but believes that what he says will happen, it will be done for him. Therefore I tell you, whatever you ask for in prayer, believe that you have received it, and it will be yours" (Mark 11:22-24).

I sensed a prompting from God to ask Him to move some mountains in my life. I felt that it was now God's timing to act. So for the first time, I felt the freedom to ask Him to do it. Since then, I have seen slow yet definite progress in the moving of each mountain.

Many people throughout history have been blessed by practicing Scripture prayer. Martin Luther's barber asked Luther what he recommended for getting closer to God and getting more out of the Word. Luther shared how he prayed through the Bible passage by passage, turning the words of God into either an adoration to offer, a confession to make, a thanksgiving to bring, or a supplication to ask.

Madame Jeanne Guyon was known for her deep spirituality and intimate relationship with God. One of her secrets was praying the Scriptures. Regarding Scripture prayer she gives these words of advice:

"Remember your main objective is to focus on God's presence."[1]

"Plunge into the very depths of the words you read until revelation, like a sweet aroma, breaks out upon you…little by little you will come to experience a very rich prayer that flows from your inward being. . . In praying the scripture you are seeking to find the Lord in what you are reading, in the very words themselves." "Once your heart has turned inwardly to the Lord, you will have an impression of his presence…. Oh, it is not that you will think about what you have read, but you will feed upon what you have read."[2]

Word Ministries Incorporated produced a book of various Scripture passages strung together by themes and turned into prayers. I do not necessarily enjoy praying the Bible in this fashion, but I do like much of what they say about the benefits of Scripture prayer:

"Prayer that brings results must be based on God's Word."[3] "Using God's Word in prayer on purpose, specifically, in prayer is one means of prayer, and it is a most effective and accurate means."[4]

"…His Word in us is the key to answered prayer—to prayer that brings results. He is able to do exceedingly abundantly above all that we ask or think, according to the power that works within us (Eph. 3:20). The power lies within God's Word. It is anointed by the Holy Spirit."[5]

"When we use God's Word in prayer we must not rush through, uttering once, and we are finished. Do not be mistaken. There is nothing 'magical' or 'manipulative' about it—no set pattern or device in order to satisfy what we want or think out of our flesh. Instead we are holding God's Word before Him. We confess what He says belongs to us."[6]

"It is not saying prayers that gets results, but it is spending time with the Father, learning His wisdom, drawing on His strength, being filled with His quietness, and basking in His love that brings results to our prayers."[7]

If you are not sure how to begin praying Scripture prayers, start by praying Paul's prayers for others as found in his letters to the churches. Pick a loved one and pray for them the same prayers Paul prayed for his beloved disciples. One of my favorites is found in Colossians:

For this reason, since the day we heard about you, we have not stopped pray-
ing for you and asking God to fill you with the knowledge of His will through
all spiritual wisdom and understanding. And we pray this in order that you
may live a life worthy of the Lord and may please Him in every way: bearing
fruit in every good work, growing in the knowledge of God, being strengthened
with all power according to His glorious might so that you may have great
endurance and patience, and joyfully giving thanks to the Father, who has
qualified you to share in the inheritance of the saints in the kingdom of light
(Colossians 1:9-12).

ENDNOTES

1. Madame Jeanne Guyon, *Experiencing God Through Prayer* (New Kensington, PA: Whitaker House, 1984), p. 17.
2. Guyon, as quoted by Richard Foster, *Devotional Classics* (San Francisco, CA: Harper Collins, 1996), pp. 321-322.
3. Word Ministries Inc, *Prayers That Avail Much* (Tulsa, OK: Harrison House, 1989), p. 13.
4. Ibid, p. 13.
5. Ibid, p. 16.
6. Ibid, p. 16.
7. Ibid, p. 19

Chapter 24

SURRENDER PRAYER

It was a defining moment. It defined not only the history of a man, but the history of every person who ever lived, lives, or will live on planet earth. Jesus was in the Garden of Gethsemane. The realization of His impending death was upon Him. He had come to understand that the end that was beckoning Him was beyond the intense physical anguish He would face dying on the cross. It would surpass the ugly emotional turmoil of rejection and abandonment. It would exceed the awful onslaught of demonic assault. It would embrace the greatest, highest, deepest, costliest spiritual price ever imagined.

Jesus, the eternal Son, would be separated from the Father. The union that stretched from eternity past would be severed. He was called upon to drink full of the cup of the wrath of Holy God poured out against the multiplied sins of the entire human race. He would experience the supreme levels of punishment and hell as He sacrificed His soul for our sins—and He did not want to do it.

Often as evangelicals we are so enamored with the deity of Jesus, the Son of God, that we overlook the reality of the humanity of Jesus, the son of Mary. We forget that He emptied Himself and set aside the glories of the godhead to become one of us so that He could die for us. Because He made it *look* so easy, we think it was so easy for Jesus. But it was not.

As a strong-willed individual I find a deep comfort in the battle of the wills that Jesus faced in the Garden. Look at the Scripture carefully:

"It is written: 'And He was numbered with the transgressors'; and I tell you that this must be fulfilled in Me. Yes, what is written about Me is reaching its fulfillment." The disciples said, "See, Lord, here are two swords." "That is enough," He replied. Jesus went out as usual to the Mount of Olives, and His

disciples followed Him. On reaching the place, He said to them, "Pray that you will not fall into temptation." He withdrew about a stone's throw beyond them, knelt down and prayed, "Father, if You are willing, take this cup from Me; yet not My will, but Yours be done." An angel from heaven appeared to Him and strengthened Him. And being in anguish, He prayed more earnestly, and His sweat was like drops of blood falling to the ground (Luke 22:37-44).

This is an awesome example of surrender prayer. In speaking of the nature of surrender prayer, one person has written, "To applaud the will of God, to do the will of God, even fight for the will of God is not difficult…until it comes at cross-purposes with our will."[1] It was over the cross that the will of the Father and the will of the Son crossed. Jesus' will was that the Father would relieve Him of the awful cup He was to drink. Yet, the Father willed otherwise. And Jesus surrendered to the Father's will.

Surrender prayer is yielding our entire will to God. It is choosing God's will over our own will. It is doing what God wants even when you don't want to. It is accepting God's way as better than our own. It is dying to something we hold dear so that God may bring it back to life and bless it, if and how He so desires (see Gen. 22). It is saying "not my will but Yours be done." It is giving permission for the seed to be put in the ground to die so it may bring forth a multiplied harvest (see John 12:24-25). It is letting go of what we deem good so that the Father may give us what He knows to be best. It is the key that frees us from the prison of self. As someone once said, it is giving all we know of ourselves to all we know of God.

———≈◉≈———

My testimony is that of running from God. Saved at an early age, I spent my early adolescent years unwilling to surrender to God. And I was miserable. I could not enjoy sin, self, rebellion, or the world. Yet, I refused to embrace God or yield my will to His.

Eventually I began to get weary of running and frustrated with fighting. One Sunday morning I was sitting in the very back row of the balcony at church.

Instead of listening to the message I was reading a Sunday school paper before going to sleep. A little quote jumped off the page and grabbed my attention: "Commitment to God is simply giving all you know of yourself to all you know of God."

I thought, *I could do that. God is much smarter than I am. Maybe I could really commit my life to Him.*

That night I decided to go to the Bible study for the high school students of our church. My friend had been bugging me to go for a while, so I went. The whole evening it seemed as though God was speaking directly to me about surrender. Would I commit all I knew of myself to all I knew of God? Would I surrender my will to His will for my life? Would I quit running *from* God and begin to run *to* and *with* Him?

I was afraid of making "just another emotional decision that would not last." So I resisted making any commitments during the meeting.

After I went home, I got alone until I could—as an act of the will beyond my emotions—surrender my life fully to God. And I did. I offered a "surrender prayer" to God. Very simply I said to God, "From this moment on I surrender my will to Your will. I commit all I know of me to all I know of You. I give you my past, present, and future. My life is a blank contract before You. My talents, relationships, interests, hopes, dreams, and future belong to You."

I was immediately staggered by the sense of peace that flooded my soul. I knew I had done the right thing. It was as though a very deep well of joy was opened in my heart. I must have smiled for two weeks straight.

That was many years ago, but even now, at least once a week I try to offer a "surrender prayer" to God. I take the eight biggest areas of my life and tell God, "I give them to You. Do with them as You see fit. I have often told You what I desire to happen in these areas, but let not *my* desire, but may *Your* will be done. You know what is best. I trust You to accomplish what You know to be best. Amen."

Every time I have sincerely made this type of surrender prayer to God, I have always felt better. So many times I see God increase His activity in these areas after I surrender them to Him.

Do you need to offer a "surrender prayer" to God? Right this moment, pause and surrender the areas of your life to God.

ENDNOTES

1. Richard Foster, Prayer: *Finding the Heart's True Home* (San Francisco, CA: Harper Collins Publishers, 1992), p. 50.

Part 5
Stretching Prayers

Chapter 25

SEVERE EMOTION PRAYER

My prayer life moved to a new depth the first time I got mad at God. I loved Him so much. I devoted so much effort to building my relationship with Him. I prayed so hard and trusted Him so deeply that I was shocked when the very thing I had prayed about going one way had gone the exact opposite direction. I felt violated. I felt that I deserved an explanation. He can do anything and yet He chose to do nothing. So I told Him how I felt.

I wept before Him. I yelled at Him. I cried out to Him. I vented my rage and pain on Him.

And I was scared to death that I had crossed a line and would be turned into a pile of ashes. I pulled my car over and sat in terrified silence waiting for thunder, lightning, and my total destruction.

But it never came.

Heaving a sigh of relief, I apologized to God for my ranting. I meekly confessed my shame at my outburst. I shook my head in embarrassment.

Then I felt it. It was a definite, discernible, spiritual hug from God. In a moment my car was full of the fatherly love of God. His still small voice reassured me that He would not turn me into ashes…this time.

In a moment I had gone from yelling at God to laughing with God.

I understood that my severe emotion prayer had touched the heart of God and He was not displeased. I sensed that it pleased Him that I cared enough to get mad. And I felt Him telling me that no matter how it looked right now, He was at work and everything would be all right.

Do you know what? Within a day the entire situation had turned around, and I had gone to a new level in my relationship with God.

Severe emotion prayer is respecting God enough to tell Him how you really feel. It is caring so much about your relationship with Him that you are willing to be honest before Him. It is obeying the admonition to pour out our hearts before Him (see Ps. 62:8).

Severe emotion prayer is one of the elements Jesus described in John 4:23-24 when He told the Samaritan woman that "true worshipers…must worship in spirit and in truth." *Spirit*, as it is used here, lacks a definite article and therefore does not refer to the Holy Spirit, but rather the human "spirit"—or in other words, "the real you." *Truth* describes reality. Therefore, severe emotion prayer can be an act of worship as you come to God bringing the real you in front of the real God. It is approaching God in absolute honesty.

When I was a recent seminary graduate (evangelically trained), I noticed that I had developed a tendency to make prayer primarily an act of the mind. When I was the pastor of a rural church, I observed my people sometimes making prayer an act of the will. But that day in my car when I got mad at God, I discovered that there is a type of prayer that is a prayer of the emotions—and not just the "nice" emotions. It is prayer of severe emotions. It is having a deep enough, familiar enough, strong enough relationship with God to bring before Him ugly severe emotions like anger, grief, disappointment, and shock.

The opposite of love is not hate. It is apathy. If we really love God and care about our relationship with Him, we will care enough to tell Him how we really feel. For many years I did not know if such honest prayer was permissible. I was taught to approach God within the comfort of Christian words and safe tones. I was not taught to approach God in absolute honesty. But as I read the Bible I saw that such honest prayer was the practice of some of those nearest to God.

Consider the Book of Job. In one day Job lost his livestock, servants, and children. Think about the grief he must have felt as his career, wealth, and family were suddenly all gone. Then, if that was not enough, he lost his health as his body became racked with painful sores. All of this occurred with not a word of explanation from God.

Three of his friends came to visit, and the first words out of Job's mouth were to curse the day he was born. It was not nice, as the ugly, pain-racked stream of raw emotion poured out of his mouth. Listen to his anguished soul cry out:

May the day of my birth perish (Job 3:3).

Why did I not perish at birth, and die as I came from the womb? (Job 3:11)

Later, Job's pain oozes out again in another torrent of raw emotion-soaked prayer. His words reek with miserable eloquence:

If only my anguish could be weighed and all my misery be placed on the scales! It would surely outweigh the sand of the seas (Job 6:2-3).

...I will not keep silent; I will speak out in the anguish of my spirit, I will complain in the bitterness of my soul (Job 7:11).

...I prefer strangling and death, rather than this body of mine (Job 7:15).

Why have You made me Your target? (Job 7:20)

At the time I first really read those words I was in the midst of a severe battle with a painful chronic illness. I was certain that God would blast Job for his emotional outburst. But God did not. It was so liberating to see in the Book of Job the model of this type of prayer.

Job's complaint was not finished in chapters 6 and 7. It continued. Listen as he vents:

I loathe my very life (Job 10:1).

Tell me what charges You have against me (Job 10:2).

Does it please You to oppress me? (Job 10:3)

Your hands shaped me and made me. Will You now turn and destroy me? (Job 10:8)

Turn away from me so I can have a moment's joy (Job 10:20).

Intimacy requires honesty. Job had an intimate relationship with God because Job was honest with God. His emotional outburst is a reflection of the depth of their relationship.

Job was a man whose reputation was that of being a man who called upon God (see Job 12:4). He obviously knew God. If you read the entire Book of Job, you find that the one opinion Job cared about was the opinion of God. To read the Book of Job is to read the emotional prayer of a man who truly loved God. Even in the midst of his most torrid emotional outbursts his loyalty to his relationship with God shines through. Amazingly he cries out:

> *I would still have this consolation—my joy in unrelenting pain—that I had not denied the words of the Holy One* (Job 6:10).

Though He slay me, yet will I hope in Him (Job 13:15).

In his classic book with the simple title of *Prayer*, O. Hallesby writes:

> "The more personal conversation is…the more it becomes real communication, a mutual exchange of ideas in which life speaks to life. So also with prayer. It should be the free, spontaneous, vital fellowship between the created person and the personal Creator, in which Life should touch life. The more that prayer becomes the untrammelled, free and natural expression of the desires of our hearts, the more real it becomes."[1]

Hallesby also writes, "[Prayer] may be an outcry from a violently agitated soul engaged in a bitter struggle."[2] If anyone ever modeled the prayer of a violently agitated soul engaged in bitter struggle, it was Jesus. He did so on at least two occasions. The first was in the Garden of Gethsemane when His sweat was as drops of blood:

> *He withdrew about a stone's throw beyond them, knelt down and prayed, "Father, if You are willing, take this cup from Me; yet not My will, but Yours be done."…And being in anguish, He prayed more earnestly, and His sweat was like drops of blood falling to the ground* (Luke 22:41-44).

The second example of Jesus' practicing severe emotion prayer was on the cross:

About the ninth hour Jesus cried out in a loud voice, "Eloi, Eloi, lama sabachthani?"—which means, "My God, my God, why have You forsaken Me?" (Matthew 27:46)

Do you love God enough to tell Him how you really feel? Have you ever appropriately expressed your deepest feelings to God? If not, why not? Maybe that's what you need to do right now.

ENDNOTES

1. O. Hallesby, *Prayer* (Minneapolis, MN: Augsburg, 1931), pp. 135-136.
2. Ibid, p. 136.

Chapter 26

SAHARA PRAYER

Have you ever tried to pray and felt nothing? Have you ever been consciously right with God, yet felt like He was a million miles away from you? Have you ever tried desperately to enter God's presence only to sense that He was hiding? Have the disciplines of the spiritual life ever become more like a duty than a delight? Has it ever felt like you were "beating on Heaven's door with bruised knuckles in the dark?"[1] Has your soul ever felt dried out from the toll of living day after day without the noticeable, refreshing sense of the presence of God? If so, you know what it is to need Sahara prayer.

Sahara prayer is continuing to seek God after He has chosen to remove the refreshment of His noticeable presence from us for a period of time. This spiritual desert period is a temporary season that purifies and deepens our faith and teaches us to love God more than the gifts He gives. Sahara prayer continues to pursue God even when He seems to be hiding from us. It will persist in waiting for, seeking after, and trusting God even though He seems to have abandoned us to experience the dark night of the soul.

An ancient Spanish writer named John describes the "dark night of the soul" as a stage of spiritual maturity where God withdraws the noticeable pleasures of His presence and leaves us feeling like we are going it alone.[2] These seasons may last a few days or a few months. The important thing is to continue to seek God through and in the midst of the dry times.

We need to realize that such dry seasons are common to all. As one fellow traveler has observed:

"The withering winds of God's hiddenness does not mean God is displeased with you, or that you are insensitive to the work of God's spirit, or that you have committed some horrendous offense against heaven, or that there is something wrong with you, or anything. Darkness is a definite experience in prayer. It is to be expected, even embraced."[3]

Another wise believer speaks with authority about these dry times. She writes:

"Don't be impatient in your times of dryness. Wait patiently for God. In doing so, your prayer life will increase and be renewed."[4]

As a relatively young Christian I found myself swallowed up in the midst of such a soul Sahara. I was at a loss for what to do. From the first moment I had surrendered my life to God, His presence had been my constant companion. One of the things I had enjoyed most about my new life was the continual feast of His presence.

One of my Christian friends told me that it was not uncommon and the real key was what I would do now. Press on or go back? If I am anything, I am persistent, so I decided to press on. Yet, I was unsure what that meant.

One day I stumbled onto an oasis in the middle of my spiritual desert. This is how it occurred. I decided to go into a literal closet and shut the door. It was pitch black in the closet. I could not see anything. I could not hear anything. There, alone in the dark, I prayed what I thought at the time was a very bold prayer.

In a strong clear voice I said, "Okay, God. I cannot see You. I cannot hear You. I cannot touch You or smell You or taste You. You seem to be hiding from me. Fine. I am going to pray anyway. Right now, I am praying solely by faith, not by feelings. In my soul I feel nothing. I am numb and dry inside. My soul is dark and barren. But You are worthy of my prayer. You are worthy of this block of time. You promise to hear and answer prayer. You promise to never leave us or forsake us. You said that without faith it is impossible to please You and those who come to You must believe that You are and that You reward those who diligently seek You.[5] So here I am, by faith, diligently seeking You."

I paused and plunged on ahead.

"I am going to bring You prayers of adoration, confession, thanksgiving, and supplication whether I feel You here today or not. I am going to pray totally by faith. So here goes. God, I adore You because…"

And before I could get the next words of praise out of my mouth I felt it. It was the refreshing splash of God's presence on my barren, dry soul. As I prayed, the presence of God filled that closet like a cloud burst. By the time I was done I was spiritually drenched. I was submerged in the replenishing water of the presence of God Himself. He had visited my closet and touched my soul.

I wish I could say that it has always been that way when I tried to pray my way out of a dry time, but that is not the case. However, often "Sahara prayers" have stirred up the cool breeze of God's presence refreshing my dry, barren soul.

Maybe you can identify closely with this chapter. Pray on by faith, not by feelings. Seek God because He is worth it, not because you feel like it, and He may just sneak up on you and refresh your soul.

E N D N O T E S

1. George Buttrick, *Prayer* (New York, NY: Abington-Cokesbury, 1942), p. 263.

2. Richard Foster, *Celebration of Discipline* (New York, NY: Harper Collins Publishers, 1978), p.102.

3. Foster, *Prayer: Finding the Heart's True Home* (New York, NY: Harper Collins Publishers, 1992), p.19.

4. Madame Jeanne Guyon, *Experiencing God Through Prayer* (New Kensington, PA: Whitaker House, 1984), p. 26.

5. Adapted from Hebrews 11:6.

Chapter 27

SECRET RENDEZVOUS PRAYER

My father is a widower. Recently he has begun to date. About once or twice a week he gets himself spruced up to take one of his lady friends to church or out to eat. When he's out on the date he has a little more spring in his step and a little more twinkle in his eye. There is something special about going out on a date.

———•———

There was a widow in my church who was in her 80s. I knew her as a rather tired, sad, whiny sort of person. One day a man from her past stopped in to see her. The next thing we knew they were dating and then got engaged. It was a great thing for her. She looked peppier, younger, and happier. Her life had changed from a black-and-white drudgery to a full-color adventure. There is something about falling in love that makes life wonderful.

———•———

When Cathy and I met, we attended a very strict Christian university. She lived off campus and I lived on campus. Neither of us owned a car. I had no access to a phone. So every time I saw her, it was a very special moment. A Friday night date with her was the absolute highlight of the week. Just thinking of Friday night got me through many a dull Greek class or a disappointing day.

Now Cathy and I have been married 22 years. Yet, our Friday dates are still the highlight of the week. Just thinking of Fridays puts a smile on my face and a spring in my step.

There is something special about going on a date with the person you love.

———•❀•———

Several years ago as I was lost in a season of Spirit-enhanced prayer, I found myself writing mushy poetry to the Lord. I was so hopelessly lavish in my expressions of love to the Lord that I was embarrassed. I was afraid I had crossed a line of inappropriate prayer and had offended God.

Then the first command came to my mind, "Love the Lord your God with all your heart soul, mind, and strength" (see Matt. 22:37-40). I understood that I was obeying this command on a different level than I ever had realized was available. During this unusual prayer time, I loved God with all my heart. I experienced a fresh level of intimacy with God. It was awesome. Love, joy, and peace flooded my heart. I experienced in a new way what it meant to be a lover of God.

Since that day, I try to occasionally enhance my time with God by viewing it as a secret rendezvous with the lover of my soul. I think of it as having something of a divine date with my delightful God. I plan a time when I can take an hour and be alone with God. I tell Him how I feel about everything and I especially take time to tell Him how much I do love Him. I listen as He reminds me of His love for me. I try to go deeper into His presence than usual and feel His love.

As I write these words, I almost shiver. I definitely smile. Just thinking of those times, those secret, special times with God, makes the hard days of life much more tolerable.

———•❀•———

Secret rendezvous prayer is a divine date with the Holy Spirit. It is taking time away from others to be alone with "the lover of your soul." It is being lavish in your expressions of your love for God. It is the prayer of pure, mutual love. It is positioning your soul to receive the drenching rain of God's love.

Maybe you never thought of prayer as the rendezvous of lovers, but it can be just as exciting (see Song of Solomon). Prayer is born and nurtured in love. After all, Jesus calls us His Bride (see Eph. 5:25-33; Rev. 19:6-8). Maybe it's new to you, but take some time to tell the Lord why you love Him so much. Do not be inhibited. Be lavish, expressive, and extravagant.

Take your time. Drink in deeply of His presence and His love. Bask in His love for you. Feel wonderfully accepted, appreciated, and cherished. Feel loved. Enjoy this moment down to the last drop.

Then tell God you will meet Him like this again, as soon as possible.

Chapter 28

SAY IT FAITH PRAYER

It was Tuesday morning of the most interesting week on planet earth since the beginning. Jesus was no longer hiding His position as Messiah. Just two days earlier He had ridden triumphantly into Jerusalem on a colt. Many had shouted Hosanna (Save!) and spread palm branches out before Him. They shouted, "Blessed is He who comes in the name of the Lord!" (Mark 11:9), and He let them.

Just one day earlier Jesus had been hungry and searched a fig tree for figs. Finding none, Jesus made a faith proclamation, cursing the fruitless fig tree saying, "No one will eat from you again" (see Mark 11:14).

Then He went into the temple on a mission. He wanted to pray but seeing the distraction caused by the moneychangers He turned over their tables and benches. Then He chased them out with a whip, proclaiming, "Is it not written: 'My house will be called a house of prayer for all nations'? But you have made it a 'den of robbers' " (Mark 11:17).

Now it was Tuesday morning and Jesus and His disciples were walking back into Jerusalem after spending the night just outside of town in Bethany. As they came upon the cursed fig tree the disciples were amazed to see it withered at its roots. Peter grabbed Jesus and said, "Rabbi, look! The fig tree You cursed has withered" (Mark 11:21).

Jesus had stated something that was not so as though it was so, and it became so. He had cursed a fig tree and it had withered from its roots in one day! Then He did something even more unusual. He looked at the tree and then at Peter and the disciples and said,

"Have faith in God," Jesus answered. "I tell you the truth, if anyone says to this mountain, 'Go, throw yourself into the sea,' and does not doubt in his heart

*but believes that what he says will happen, it will be done for him. Therefore
I tell you, whatever you ask for in prayer, believe that you have received it, and
it will be yours"* (Mark 11:22-24).

And just like that, Jesus introduced the disciples to a new type of prayer: "Say
it faith prayer." This is one of the most powerful types of prayer available. It can
wither fig trees and move mountains. In another passage Jesus said it has the power
to uproot mulberry trees (see Luke 17:6).

I had never really heard of this type of prayer until one night author Elmer
Towns was speaking at the church I attended as a college student. Just a year or two
earlier God had called me to plant a new church with a team of other students. I
had spoke about this often with God but never with others. I had been afraid to
go public with such an audacious thought. I was not even a pastoral ministries
major. (I majored in counseling.) I am an introvert. No one would have thought it
possible. Planting a church was a mountainous thing that was beyond the realm of
possibility for me.

Yet, as Dr. Towns spoke about "say it faith," God spoke to me. Towns defined
"say it faith" as "the supernatural ability of God whereby He plants in the human
heart the gift to trust Him for marvelous results in Christian service."[1] As he spoke,
God reaffirmed my calling to plant a church and convicted me of my need to
express it aloud, in public, to others. Until this time, because no one knew, I could
always bail out at a difficult point. But Dr. Towns and, more importantly, the Holy
Spirit impressed me with the absolute necessity of saying what my mountain was
and telling it to be removed. Then the invitation was given to walk down the aisle
to the front of the church and tell one of the pastors what mountains we believed
God would move by faith.

It was a long, slow walk down that aisle to shake the hand of the smiling pastor. He looked at me expectantly and I nearly gagged on the words. In a quivering
voice I whispered, "I am going to plant a healthy, growing, multiplying church in
Columbus, Ohio." He leaned closer and asked me to speak up.

Trying to sound louder and more confident I tried again, "I am going to plant
a healthy, growing, multiplying church in Columbus, Ohio. It is a great church."

It was better the second time, but I doubt if he was convinced or remembers that night. But I do, and God does, and that's all that matters.

In response to the calling and prompting of God, I had stated something that was not so as though it was so and it became so. Today there is a healthy, growing, multiplying church in Columbus, Ohio. We have several thousand members, 65 acres of land, and millions of dollars of facilities. We have planted several other healthy churches. People are saved regularly and over a hundred people are baptized every year. A mountainous task has been performed by faith. The impossible, or at least highly improbable, has become actual. What was just a dream in my heart and words on my tongue has become a reality.

From that night on the church became real to me. I prayed about the new church in a different way. It was no longer a "what if" but a "what will be." I began to see it more clearly in my mind. I could feel it more deeply in my heart. In my heart I could hear the people joined in singing praise to God. I could envision people responding to the invitation to be saved. I pictured people meeting in homes to study the Bible.

Once I stated my faith, God began to move the mountain. Before long I had a team to go with me. We discovered in which part of Columbus we were to plant the church. I got a better job and was able to save more money. Doors began to open providing me with more opportunities to learn what I needed to know. I was given more opportunities to minister. My confidence began to grow. My prayer life became more bold and effective. I doubt if any of that would have happened if I had not begun to practice "say it faith prayer."

------=≫‹(◉)›≪=------

Say it faith prayer is calling down the will of God to earth (see Matt. 6:10b). It is boldly proclaiming in prayer what God has shown you He will do in a situation (see James 5:14-15). It is cooperating with God in moving giant mountains and deeply rooted mulberry trees through the power of verbalized, faith-filled prayer. It is stating something that was not so as though it is so in order that God may make it so.

Of all the types of prayer described in this book, for most of us "say it faith prayer" may be the most rare. There are those unique people with a great gift of faith who practice this type of prayer more frequently. But for most of us, it is an uncommon occasion when we know the will of God so clearly that we have the liberty to call it into reality. But it must be available more often than we use it. I say this because of the number of times Jesus encourages us to "say it faith prayer" in the Gospels (see Matt. 17:20; 21:21-22; Mark 11:22-24; Luke 17:6).

I have learned that faith is not faith until it is expressed and/or acted upon. "Say it faith" is expressing faith in God: His person, His promises, and His power.

I have made many faith declarations as a pastor. Before they became a reality I declared that our church would own land, build a sanctuary, build a gym, plant churches, and have over a thousand a week in attendance. Say it faith works.

Has God laid something on your heart that He is waiting for you to believe? Is there a mountain He is telling you to move? Is there a mulberry tree He is showing you that He is ready to cast in the sea? Is there a fig tree He wants to wither? Do you need to say it?

Maybe you need to express your faith by writing it on your prayer list or in your prayer journal. Maybe you need to express your faith by praying it aloud with a prayer partner. Maybe you need to make a verbal declaration or testimony in a public setting.

ENDNOTES

1. Elmer Towns, *Say-It-Faith* (Wheaton, IL: Tyndale House Publishers, 1983), p. 19.

Chapter 29

SAY NO TO FOOD PRAYER

Desperate situations demand desperate measures. Hannah's situation had reached the crisis point. Her womb was barren and her heart was broken. In her culture a barren woman was a third-class citizen. Her husband had two wives. The other wife had children and never failed to use this fact to provoke Hannah. Hannah's biological clock was ticking. She needed action and she needed it now.

That year when her family made their annual trip to worship the Lord in Shiloh, Hannah was so desperate and distraught that she could not and would not eat. She went to the tabernacle and cried out her anguish to God. She vowed that if the Lord would give her a son, she would give him back to the Lord. Then she sensed that God had heard her plea and she ate.

Very soon afterward, Hannah became pregnant and bore a son whom she named Samuel. The name *Samuel* means "heard by the Lord" because he was the answer to her "so desperate she was willing to say no to food prayer."

What Hannah practiced was "say no to food prayer." Saying no to food prayer is prayer combined with fasting.[1] It is allowing your desperation to overwhelm your appetite for food. It is taking your attention from the physical in order to give your attention to the spiritual. It is letting God know that you are so serious about Him and your prayer needs that you won't eat. It is fasting in secret so that God may reward you openly. It is saying "no" to food in order to say "yes" to God.

———— ·◉· ————

A friend of mine named Rhonda had had no contact with her adult daughter, Megan, for several years. A few years ago, Rhonda became a part of a church and returned to God after a couple of decades of distance. Soon she discovered a renewed burden to connect with her daughter. One Sunday morning she heard a message on the power of prayer and fasting. She had become desperate to see her daughter again after all the years of separation. At this point she realized she had nothing to lose, so she gave "say no to food prayer" a try.

She began her fast on Monday and sought God with desperate prayer each day. On Thursday evening she got a phone call. It was Megan. After all those years, she wanted to get together with her mom. (By the way, I saw Megan and Rhonda walking into church together last Sunday!)

———⹁⟨⟨◉⟩⟩⹁———

Jesus taught that "say no to food prayer" was to be a regular discipline in the life of His disciples. As part of the Sermon on the Mount, Jesus spoke of "when," not "if," we fast. This is because saying no to food is an expected part of the life of those who follow after Christ.

> *"When you fast, do not look somber as the hypocrites do, for they disfigure their faces to show men they are fasting. I tell you the truth, they have received their reward in full. But when you fast, put oil on your head and wash your face, so that it will not be obvious to men that you are fasting, but only to your Father, who is unseen; and your Father, who sees what is done in secret, will reward you* (Matthew 6:16-18).

Jesus taught that after He, the heavenly Bridegroom, ascended to Heaven, fasting was to become a regular discipline in the life of His disciples:

> *Jesus answered, "How can the guests of the bridegroom mourn while he is with them? The time will come when the bridegroom will be taken from them; then they will fast* (Matthew 9:15).

Notice the last four words of the verse, "then they will fast."

I began to practice "say no to food prayer" when I was in college. I gave God one day a week and used my meal times to pray. This practice is one I have followed ever since. There have been periods when I have gotten away from it, but I always return because I have experienced so many answers to my "say no to food prayers."

Several years ago I studied every verse in the Bible related to "say no to food prayer" and fasting. I was amazed at how many miracles were preceded by "say no to food prayer." I was thrilled to find the huge amount of awesome benefits available to the person who practices "say no to food prayer." Read through this list and see which of these benefits stirs you to consider saying no to food in order to pray:

1. *Hold back God's judgment* (Deut. 9:18-26)
2. *Gain victory* (Judg. 20:26,35; 2 Chron. 20:3-4,12,15)
3. *Get God's protection* (Ezra 8:21-23)
4. *Receive God's plan* (Neh. 1:4)
5. *Save a nation* (Esther 4:3,16)
6. *Empathize with a sufferer* (Ps. 35:14)
7. *Humble yourself* (Ps. 69:10)
8. *Please God and do more* (Isa. 58:6-14)
9. *Receive revelation from God* (Dan. 10:2-3)
10. *Return to God* (Joel 2:12)
11. *Prepare for the return of Christ* (Joel 2; Luke 5:33-35)
12. *Repent* (Jon. 3:5-9)
13. *Cast out demons* (Matt. 17:21)
14. *Prepare for greater impact* (Luke 4)
15. *Get prayers heard* (Acts 10:30-31)
16. *Select missionaries* (Acts 13:1-4)
17. *Select leaders* (Acts 14:23)
18. *Give yourself to prayer* (1 Cor. 7:3-5)

Saying no to food in order to pursue God in desperate prayer is a type of prayer that has seen renewed interest as we are living in what many believe to be the end-times. Fasting and prayer has so many potentially powerful benefits that it can be recommended for a variety of reasons.[2] Maybe there is a situation in your life that has reached the desperation point. Or better yet, maybe you want to deal with a situation before it reaches the desperation point. Why not set aside a meal or a day or a few days to seek the Lord about your situation with "say no to food prayer"?

ENDNOTES

1. Fasting, as used in the Bible, means "self-denial." Fasting is choosing not to partake of food because spiritual hunger is so deep, determination in intercession is so intense, or spiritual warfare so demanding that you temporarily set aside even fleshly needs to give yourself more wholly to prayer. A normal fast involves fasting from all food, but not from water (see Matt. 4:2). Typically fasting went for one complete 24-hour period, usually from sundown to sundown. The early Church fasted two days every week, Wednesday and Friday. Other biblical fasts went from 3 to 40 days. Both individual and corporate fasts are seen in the Scriptures. Fasting may also include skipping a meal consistently or abstaining from certain foods or activities. Some of my favorite quotes about the benefits of fasting include:

"When you make a choice to fast, you strengthen yourself to stand against a force that has enslaved your spiritual appetite…. You never gain an outward victory over sin, until you take inner responsibility for your actions."—*Elmer Towns*

"I believe the power of fasting as it relates to prayer is the spiritual atomic bomb of our moment in history to bring down the strongholds of evil, bring a great revival and spiritual awakening to America, and accelerate the fulfillment of the Great Commission." —*Bill Bright, Campus Crusade*

"Fasting is designed to make prayer mount up as eagle's wings. It is intended to usher the supplicant into the audience chamber of the King and to extend to him the golden scepter. It may be expected to drive back the oppressive process of darkness and loosen their hold on the prayer objective. It is calculated to give an edge to man's intercessions and power to his petitions. Heaven is ready to bend its ear and listen when someone prays with fasting." *—Arthur Wallis*

"Fasting shows the seriousness of our commitment. When we step into fasting we say, 'God you have to move. You have got to do it.' " *—Kay Arthur*

"Fasting produces a work of art—the tempered, selfless Christian—that can be created through no other process of refinement." *—Leo Buerno*

"It is not that God speaks louder when we fast, but we begin to hear Him better." *—Julio Ruibal*

"Fasting is the foundry by which we are purified." *—Leo Buerno*

"Fasting helps express, to deepen, to confirm the resolution that we are ready to sacrifice everything, [even] ourselves to attain that which we seek for the kingdom of God." *—Andrew Murray*

Chapter 30

SURVIVAL PRAYER

King David had been removed from his post, chased from his home, and forced to leave his country. He was trying to hide in the nation of his greatest enemies. But unfortunately he was discovered, captured, and taken to the one Philistine he did not want to see, Achish.

Achish, the Philistine king of Gath, could not get over his good fortune. David had killed Gath's greatest hero, Goliath. David had killed 200 Philistines as a dowry to marry the daughter of Israel's King Saul. David had led several victorious battles against the Philistines. And now David, his arch enemy and Israel's hero, had fallen into his hands, alone and unarmed (see 1 Samuel 17–21).

David surveyed his hopeless situation and did something he had done before. He prayed a very simple prayer, "Help!" (see Ps. 56:9). God helped. And David escaped.

Maybe you grew up with the notion that prayer needed to sound impressive. (My mother grew up as a Quaker and the prayers of her family were in King James English. As a boy I always thought that was impressive). Maybe you have been taught that prayers need to be long to be effective. (One Sunday morning my family was visiting a church in another state. My boys timed one of the many lofty pastoral prayers to be nearly ten minutes long. It seemed longer. My boys were impressed with the length, but not the prayer.) Possibly you have picked up the notion that prayers need to be given in a deep baritone voice and be chock full of multi-syllable theological terms. Forget it! There are times when the situation is so desperate and the need is so urgent that a simple prayer of survival is in order:

"Help!" Now say it aloud, "Help!" Survival prayer is crying out to God at the point of utter desperation. It is coming boldly to the throne of grace, asking God to help at a time of intense need. It is coming to God when no one else can, or will.

The Psalms are full of examples of the survival prayer. Notice the word "help" in each of these passages. (I had it printed in bold type so you would not miss it.)

For God is our refuge and strength, an ever-present **help** *in trouble. Therefore we will not fear, though the earth give way and the mountains fall into the heart of the sea* (Psalm 46:1-2).

I lift up my eyes to the hills—where does my **help** *come from? My* **help** *comes from the Lord, the Maker of heaven and earth* (Psalm 121:1-2).

Come quickly to **help** *me, O Lord my Savior* (Psalm 38:22).

Be pleased, O Lord, to save me; O Lord, come quickly to **help** *me* (Psalm 40:13).

Then my enemies will turn back when I call for **help**. *By this I will know that God is for me* (Psalm 56:9).

Hasten, O God, to save me; O Lord, come quickly to **help** *me* (Psalm 70:1).

Yet I am poor and needy; come quickly to me, O God. You are my **help** *and my deliverer; O Lord, do not delay* (Psalm 70:5).

Help *us, O God our Savior, for the glory of Your name; deliver us and forgive our sins for Your name's sake* (Psalm 79:9).

Our **help** *is in the name of the Lord, the Maker of heaven and earth* (Psalm 124:8).

Too often we get the idea that God is not interested in this type of prayer. Yet, the opposite is true.[1] The Bible encourages survival prayer when it states: "Let us then approach the throne of grace with confidence, so that we may receive mercy and find grace to help us in our time of need" (Heb. 4:16).

True survival prayer is offered by God-dependent people who are in desperate situations and have nowhere else to turn. They have done all they could do or there is simply nothing else they can do. So they cry out to God for help.

Survival prayer is wonderful not only because it is so simple; it also is wonderful because it gets results.

When Judah's King Asa's army was outnumbered two to one, Asa offered the survival prayer:

Then Asa called to the Lord his God and said, "Lord, there is no one like You to help the powerless against the mighty. Help us, O Lord our God, for we rely on You, and in Your name we have come against this vast army. O Lord, You are our God; do not let man prevail against You" (2 Chronicles 14:11).

God hears and answers survival prayers. He gave Asa wonderful results:

The Lord struck down the Cushites before Asa and Judah. The Cushites fled, and Asa and his army pursued them as far as Gerar. Such a great number of Cushites fell that they could not recover; they were crushed before the Lord and His forces. The men of Judah carried off a large amount of plunder (2 Chronicles 14:12-13).

Daniel heard that his prayer life would lead to being thrown into the lions' den. So he asked God for help:

*Then these men went as a group and found Daniel praying and asking God for **help*** (Daniel 6:11).

God hears and answers survival prayers. He gave Daniel wonderful results:

My God sent His angel, and He shut the mouths of the lions. They have not hurt me, because I was found innocent in His sight. Nor have I ever done any wrong before you, O king" (Daniel 6:22).

When Jonah ran from God and was thrown from the ship in the midst of a terrible storm he offered a survival prayer. God heard his cry for help and sent a great fish to swallow Jonah. The fish kept Jonah from being drowned and took him where he was supposed to have gone in the first place, Nineveh.

*But the Lord provided a great fish to swallow Jonah, and Jonah was inside the fish three days and three nights. From inside the fish Jonah prayed to the Lord his God. He said: "In my distress I called to the Lord, and He answered me. From the depths of the grave I called for **help**, and You listened to my cry"* (Jonah 1:17–2:2).

The disciples were out in a boat during a storm and saw Jesus coming to them walking on the water. Peter took a step of faith and walked toward Jesus on the water. But he looked at the wind, became afraid, and began to sink. He offered a modified survival prayer when he cried, "Lord, save me" (see Matt. 14:22-32).

Jesus heard and answered his survival prayer: "Immediately Jesus reached out His hand and caught him. 'You of little faith,' He said, 'why did you doubt?' And when they climbed into the boat, the wind died down" (Matt. 14:31-32).

I do not think the Bible advocates living your life in crisis mode. I do not think it encourages us to pray this prayer all the time, every day. But when we are in a desperate situation, when we have done what we can do, when we have nowhere else to turn, when the crisis comes so quickly there is no other option—then it is time to prayer the survival prayer. "Help!"[2]

Are there some areas of your life that are beyond your control? Do you face situations too complex for you to unravel? Is it a problem that is much bigger than you can handle? Have you tried everything else? Is it a matter of survival? Then it is time to offer the survival prayer. Say it with me, "Help!"

ENDNOTES

1. O. Hallesby in his classic book *Prayer* has written, "Prayer and helplessness are inseparable. Only he who is helpless can truly pray." (Minneapolis, MN: Augsburg Publishing House, 1931), p. 17.

2. "Your helplessness is the most powerful plea which rises up to the tender father-heart of God. He has heard your prayer from the very first moment that you honestly cried to Him your need" (Hallesby, p. 19).

Chapter 31

STICKING IT OUT PRAYER

On August 18, 1991, I woke up with a horrible case of the flu. This flu hung on as I lost 18 pounds in three weeks. I began to feel a terrible, steady pain in my joints and muscles. The slightest bit of cold air made it all the worse. I carried around a giant headache that would not go away. Suddenly I was allergic to all sorts of things. My cognitive capacities would sometimes short-circuit as I could see words in my head but had great difficulty getting them to come out of my mouth. (This is not a good thing if you are a pastor.) I could not sleep for more than a few hours at a time. Strangely, about five o'clock every evening I would get a terrible sore throat and begin to feel like waves of despair were crashing on the beach of my soul.

Yet, none of that could compare with the crushing fatigue that I felt, which was like wearing cement and trying to run underwater. I woke up exhausted and stayed exhausted all day long. I would to lie in bed and concentrate on mustering all of my strength so I could turn over by myself. I had been a varsity athlete in college, and yet, at one point I was so weak the only thing I could do all day was crawl down the hall to the bathroom.

On top of that my three boys were all under the age of five. They just could not understand why Dad could not play with them like he used to or why he could not go out and make a snowman.

Beyond that, my church was going through a difficult period of transition. As the senior pastor it was important that I invest additional energy in helping navigate the church through the challenging waters it faced. Yet, I did not have any extra energy.

But worse than that was the awful guilt I felt. With three little boys, my wife really needed me to help out around the house and with the children. Yet, it was all I could do to take care of myself and try to keep working. I hated to see that my exhaustion was wearing her out.

I lived like that for ten months before I told anyone or sought help. Eventually I was diagnosed with chronic fatigue immune deficiency syndrome–CFIDS for short. (My male ego was hurt when I found out that it is an illness contracted most frequently by overachieving females.) CFIDS at that time was an illness few people understood.

I was frustrated from being the slave of my pain and fatigue. I was frustrated because I was a goal-oriented person who was now unable to pursue any goal other than survival. I was frustrated because when I was home I did not have the strength to get off the couch to play with my boys. I was frustrated because my fatigue was wearing my wife out.

But more than anything I was frustrated with God. The only response I could get from Him was silence…blank, empty, hollow, deafening silence. Day after day I asked for deliverance, for at least an explanation, or at the very least a time frame for my agony. (I looked in the Book of Job for a time frame. How long did he suffer? I even asked some of the best Bible scholars in the country that question, and they all had the same answer, "The Bible does not say.") Yet, day after day, week after week, month after month, God said nothing. My illness stretched into years, yet on this issue I received only silence.

For a time I prayed on diligently, an hour a day for months. Yet God was still silent. It felt like He had abandoned me and I did not even know why. My soul was dry and my heart broken. I hate to admit it, but eventually I reasoned that if God would no longer speak to me then I would not speak to Him, and for a period of weeks I had almost no prayer life.

But I knew this was wrong. I am a Christian and Christians "cannot not" pray. I am a child of God and children of God "cannot not" talk to their heavenly Father.

So, little by little, I began to practice saying thanks prayers and then singing praises prayers. Then I did a little selfish intercessory prayers and sorrow over my sin prayers. And I felt a little better.

Then one day I got a card from my mom. My mom had plenty of health problems of her own, yet did not let it stop her. The essence of her card said, "Quit griping and get going again." As I read it I almost laughed out loud. I had come way too far with God in my life to give up on Him now. So finally I began to tell God I would love Him and serve Him *even if.*

Even if I never got well.

Even if He never answered my prayers.

Even if He never gave me any explanation.

And a funny thing happened. I began to get noticeably better.

Getting better has been a very slow process. It has been almost 12 years since I first got sick and I still battle CFIDS every day. But I am still getting better. I exercise almost an hour a day. I run three miles, three times a week. My wife and I frequently take up to a 30-mile bike rides on my day off. And the pain is much better.

But even if I was not getting better, even if I only got worse, God would still be worth my loyalty and love. I deserve eternal death and He has given me eternal life and abundant life. Even if He never said another thing to me, did another thing for me, gave another thing to me, He would still deserve all of the love and devotion I can give Him.

And one day I will be "all better." When I say, "better" I mean, "better!" I will walk the streets of Heaven in a brand-new, pain-free, tireless, non-allergic, glorious, incorruptible body. No more fatigue! No more weakness! No more exhaustion! No more pain! I not only will be "as good as I used to be," but I will be much better than I ever imagined!

———◦◉◦———

Sticking it out prayer is expressing your loyalty to God in the face of His discipline, silence, or hard-to-understand ways. It is refusing to hold a grudge toward

God. It is getting knocked down and coming back for more. It is stating that you trust Him enough to let Him take you beyond what you thought you could bear. It is returning unconditional loyalty for God's gift of unconditional love.

Job obviously practiced sticking it out prayer when, in the midst of his anguish, he said, "Though He slay me, yet will I hope in Him" (Job 13:15).

Sticking it out prayer is like standing on the edge of a high diving board or at the top of a ski hill. It evokes feelings of both wild fear and liberating adventure. There is something deeply satisfying about it. I have come to appreciate it so much that I offer "sticking it out, *even if,* prayers" almost every day.

Maybe there is a very specific area where you need to offer a sticking it out prayer. It could be, "Lord, I will love and serve You even if:

…my mate does not change.

…my dreams do not come true.

…I do not get the promotion.

…my mother is not healed.

…my child does not get born again.

…my prayers are not answered.

…I never meet 'Mr. or Miss Right.'

…I am never given an explanation for the adversity I am facing."

Let me encourage you to offer your own sticking it out prayer right now.

Additional copies of this book and other
book titles from DESTINY IMAGE are
available at your local bookstore.

For a bookstore near you, call 1-800-722-6774

Send a request for a catalog to:

Destiny Image® Publishers, Inc.
P.O. Box 310
Shippensburg, PA 17257-0310

"Speaking to the Purposes of God for This
Generation and for the Generations to Come"

For a complete list of our titles,
visit us at www.destinyimage.com